History
of
CSWs

Communication
Support
Workers

History
of
CSWs
Communication
Support
Workers

Foreword by Chris Green

Maria Bailey &
Andrew Owen

TALK WITH SIGN BOOKS Ltd, GLOUCESTERSHIRE

HISTORY OF CSWs
© Maria Bailey & Andrew Owen 2012

First published in 2012 by
TALK WITH SIGN BOOKS Ltd
9 Churchill Way
Mitcheldean
Gloucestershire
GL17 0AZ
United Kingdom

Website: www.talkwithsign.com

ISBN 978-0-9572510-0-7

Cover design by Andrew Owen

Printed by KnowledgePoint Limited, Reading.

Contents

Foreword: Chris Green

In nineteen seventy something I happened to be staying with a Deaf friend in San Francisco. In the days before the Disability Rights Act was enforced, even in America, Marlon Kuntze was an activist in the Independent Living movement. One day he took me out in his beaten up old Volkswagen camper van and parked up in a disused gas station in Oakland. After a few minutes a large truck pulled in beside us and the black driver signed to me to wind my window down upon which a large crumpled brown paper supermarket bag was thrust at me. The truck drove off immediately with a squealing of wheels. Marlon signed at me to open the bag - it was full of money. Bills of various denominations - hundreds of dollars worth spilled out onto my lap. I asked him what, why, where from? He told me it was a contribution to the Deaf cause from the radical Black Panther movement.

This episode made me realise that in order to further a cause it takes a fusion of different factors. Progress is rarely made by a single event or by a single individual, nor is it made by a single institution acting alone. As Warren Nickerson and I discovered more than twenty years ago, all of these things need to come together at the right moment and that right moment is a result of the mood of the nation at the time, something we call the zeitgeist. The role of the communicator evolved from many things that were happening at the time – disability rights, youth unemployment, Deaf emancipation, education reform and a host of new legislation all contributed to the context of developing services for Deaf students. In tracing the history of Communication Support Workers, the book you are about to read evidences all of these factors and more.

Alliances the Key

Like the Black Panthers lending their support and experience to the Deaf of America, so the National Association for Tertiary Education for Deaf People (NATED) helped create loose alliances between some unusual bedfellows for the good of the cause. The Royal National Institute for the Deaf (RNID), British Deaf Association (BDA), National Deaf Children's Society (NDCS), National Bureau for Students with Disabilities (SKILL), National Council for Social Workers with the Deaf (NCSWD) were all involved to some extent in lobbying the Manpower Services Commission (MSC), Members of Parliament and Local Education Authorities about the plight of Deaf trainees. The pressure eventually persuaded the government to make special provision for disabled trainees. I remember in 1985 getting some raised eyebrows at the British Association of Teachers of the Deaf (BATOD) conference in London whilst standing on stage and literally kicking away the foundation blocks of a cardboard educational pyramid to demonstrate the need for support in post 16 education as well as Youth Training Scheme (YTS) training. The result was to create yet another ally with an influential body.

Of course, much has happened since Warren and I put fingers to keyboard over twenty years ago, not least in the area of advances in technology. Cochlear implants, smart phones, email, You Tube, Skype, voice to text translators and social media are all contributing to change the role of the communicator. There are parallels however – current high youth unemployment mirrors the situation in the 1980s and recent proposals from all sides of the political spectrum are calling for increased apprenticeships, work placements and vocational training opportunities for young people. If history is repeating itself, perhaps now is the time to wave the equal opportunities banner and suggest that if young Deaf people are included in these schemes, who will be there to support them?

As well as charting the progress of CSWs with respect to institutions, legislation and qualifications, more importantly perhaps, this book highlights the vital part played by many of the individuals involved. Views, comments and reports from a variety of professionals working with and for Deaf people are freely given, warts and all. There are representations from management figures as well as those working 'at the chalk face' and most important of all – the opinions of Deaf people themselves.

Continually Updating

It seems that every time I switch on my computer these days there is something that I am obliged to update. Well, by those standards the book that Warren and I wrote way back in 1992 is well overdue an update! But this book is more than that, it tells the story of Communication Support Workers and answers questions such as 'what happened next?' and 'where are they now?' It tracks the progress of the service through two decades of developments. There are triumphs and set-backs, successes and failures but through it all CSWs have continued to hold a vital position in facilitating the access of Deaf students to post 16 education and training.

This book tracks the development of CSWs from their early birth to the latest bid for a nationally recognised qualification.

Chris Green
Bakewell, March 2012

Introduction

The inspiration for writing this book happened during the process of developing the professional qualification for Communication Support Workers by Signature as part of the government funded I-Sign Project, between 2009 and 2011. Once the qualification had finally achieved accreditation and the National Occupational Standards (NOS) had been approved and finalised, we both felt such a sense of achievement that we agreed that we needed to share this journey with others. Another important factor was that only one text book which concentrated solely on the role of the CSW had ever been published. This book, 'The Rise of The Communicator' by Chris Green and Warren Nickerson had been published in 1992 and had, unfortunately, been out of print for a number of years. This presented an ideal opportunity to publish a new work.

We realised that if we took the date of the first qualified CSWs entering the workforce as 1987, being the end of the first communicator training course, and completed this book in 2012, it would, in our opinion, be a fitting tribute to mark twenty five years of qualified CSWs in the workplace; the Silver Jubilee of the CSW. Our goal was to complete the book by the summer of 2012 and to hold the book launch at the annual conference of NATED (The National Association for Tertiary Education for the Deaf) and ACSW (The Association of Communication Support Workers), on 30th June 2012.

Interviewing People Who Were There

Initial discussions led to us agreeing that an appropriate way to gather information would be to interview people who were 'there' at significant times over the last twenty five years. For example, we considered that it would be very interesting to trace some of the early CSWs - those who undertook the initial training courses in the late 1980s, along with people who were involved in developing these courses and people who taught on the courses; people who were working in the field of Deaf education at this time etc. This seemed an appropriate method of carrying out our research. We were both amazed and humbled at the number of people who agreed to share their experiences and memories with us. We were fortunate that we were indeed able to interview some of the early CSW students and hear their version of their training and what it felt like to be among the very first qualified CSWs. We also included a section at the end of each report entitled 'Where are you now?' We wanted to find out how many (if any) of those original CSWs from the late 1980s had remained in the profession. Very soon, word of our project began to spread and we were being contacted by people telling us of their roles in the history of CSWs and asking if we wanted to interview them. The research took us across the length and breadth of the UK. We gave people the choice of being interviewed face-to-face;

by telephone or Skype. Interviews were recorded, transcribed and then written in report formats. Everyone interviewed was involved in the process and gave their agreement to the final reports which appear in this book.

We made use of journal articles, research papers and literature previously published concerning CSWs and their role. Not all were complimentary, but we wanted to give a balanced view of the information available to us. However, as CSWs ourselves, we felt that we were in a position to be able to comment and give our opinions also. Therefore we have included sections from our own perspectives because we were 'there' too at significant times. We discussed at length what convention to use when referring to Deaf people. Throughout this book the word 'Deaf' is used to refer to (people with) any range of deafness, from mild to profound, and we offer our apologies to any who disapprove.

A Rocky Road

The role of the CSW over the last twenty five years and the path to seeking the recognition it so justly deserves has not been smooth. In many ways it has been a hard-fought battle – a profession strewn with controversy at the outset, and with a debate that still continues.

This book is an attempt to chart the journey and give reports from many of the people who were there at the crucial points in time. It also attempts to provide a contemporary political view, describe the struggles for recognition and respect, and presents a summing-up of the situation in the year of the CSW Silver Jubilee.

We are acutely aware that this book is a collaboration rather than the work of only two people. Other experts have given their time, have been open with their views, and have been willing to edit and agree each of their portions of this book. They are as much our co-authors, for which we offer our profound thanks. We believe that this book represents a valuable record of the twenty five years during which the role of the CSW has come of age, from the perspective of a number of people who were actively involved in the journey. We hope you enjoy it.

Acknowledgements

We are indebted to a number of people who gave freely of their time and shared their experiences with us. Without them, we would not have been able to uncover so much of the variety and specifics of the history of Communication Support Workers. Sincere apologies to anyone whose name has been inadvertently omitted – we value the input of everyone, so thank you one and all:

Judith Collins, Celine Crowley, Jim Edwards, Chris Green, Emma Green, Michelle Jones, Peter Llewellyn-Jones, Tracey Kelsall, Karen Nicholson, Sean Nicholson, Miranda Pickersgill, Tracey Pycroft, Nicola Richards, Rob Rogers and Cath Smith.

A special thanks to our expert proofreaders Claire Bailey, Wendy Martin and Hilary Hodgson. Your feedback and observations played a crucial part in the journey.

Thanks also go to our families, friends and colleagues for your help, patience and encouragement, without which we would not have been able to complete this book.

Maria Bailey and Andy Owen
June 2012

1 In The Beginning: Background

The years preceding the launch of the initial training courses for Communication Support Workers, originally referred to as communicators, in the mid 1980s, were vitally important in terms of understanding why such a role needed to be created. Some of the events from these years are now explained in the hope that readers can fully appreciate the background to the 'rise of the communicator' and to put everything that followed thereafter into context. Stewart Simpson (2007) explains:

'Prior to the 1970s few, very few Deaf people entered further or higher education. It was not expected they would. Those who were profoundly Deaf and who had attended a specialist school for the Deaf left school at the age of sixteen with, on average, a reading age in single figures. There was no established system of support in colleges of further education, and much reliance for their post-16 training and employment was placed on specialist social workers with the Deaf. It was they who sought to find work for young Deaf people. It was the social worker who gave interpreting support at interviews, on the first day at work, at health and safety lectures, trades unions meetings, and on day release courses. The system was not uniform, not comprehensive and certainly not universal. It depended on the goodwill and other commitments of individual social workers usually employed by local voluntary organisations' (Simpson, 2007, p173).

It should also be made clear that, at that time, sign language was not as prominent as it is today. Also, formal training for interpreters had not been established. This was not to happen until the late 1970s. Until then all communication support for Deaf people was provided by either social workers for the Deaf or, in education, Teachers of the Deaf. In her report in chapter 6, Cath Smith recalls the feeling that no one consulted Deaf people about the introduction of interpreters. Most Deaf people were happy to use social workers for doctor's appointments etc. They felt comfortable and knew their social workers, but interpreters were a new breed. It would take time for Deaf people to understand the difference between a social worker and an interpreter.

Interpreters Needed, Not Social Workers

Conversely, Simpson (2007) records that, by the 1970s Deaf people were beginning to exercise their rights to equality and access to services and opportunities normally available to hearing people. Leaders in the Deaf community argued that they (Deaf people) were not a social problem, they did not need social workers. They claimed that they had a communication problem in a hearing world and therefore, what they needed were interpreters. Put simply, at that time, the Missioner/Welfare Officer provided social work, community work and interpreting. As more and more Deaf people sought greater opportunities and equality, it became clear that separate roles would be needed.

Historically many local authorities continued to use an oral policy of education for Deaf children, and sign language was banned. This was a legacy of the Milan Congress in 1880, when schools for the Deaf in Britain and Europe which had previously used sign language in Deaf education quickly adopted the oral method. Sign language in British Deaf schools was gradually forced underground as the reaction in support of the Oralist movement strengthened (Milan 1880 [online, n.d.]). Even today, many Deaf adults recall how they were forced to sit on their hands in class to stop them from using sign language to communicate with each other. Taking this into account, it is quite easy to understand the claim that there was such a low academic expectation for Deaf students. It is now widely accepted that Deaf students are no less able to achieve academically than their non Deaf peers, if they are provided with appropriate access to education in order to help them to achieve their full potential.

The beginning of a revival came in the early 1970s when William Stokoe proved that sign language (in this case American sign language) was a language in its own right with its own grammar, vocabulary, structure and syntax (Milan 1880 [online, n.d.]). Sign language was reborn.

This then coincided in the 1980s, with an increase in the demand from young Deaf people of all abilities, to enter further and higher education.

The Manpower Services Commission (MSC) was established in 1973 as a non-departmental public body of the Department of Employment Group. The MSC's aim was to co-ordinate employment and training services through a ten-member commission drawn from industry, trade unions, local authorities and education interests. Recession and rising unemployment dampened these aspirations somewhat, but a range of schemes were introduced, including the Youth Training Scheme (YTS) which, at least temporarily, helped to reduce the number of young people claiming unemployment benefit at the time (Simpson, 2007).

In the 1970s and early 1980s, prior to the introduction of YTS, other newly formed MSC sponsored training schemes opened up entirely new avenues into Further Education colleges. At this time, specialist support services for Deaf students barely existed. Many young students were directed into 'Mode BII' Schemes which were described as discrete schemes for 'disabled' young people. Green and Nickerson (1992) describe these schemes as dumping grounds for young people who required non-existent special assistance if they were to be able to access a regular scheme. Many young Deaf students were enrolled on such schemes.

One such example was given by Celine Crowley who recalls studying on a catering course at Bournville College, Birmingham between 1980 and 1982. Twelve young students, all Deaf, were enrolled on the course. The tutor was hearing and Celine recalls that none of the students understood what they were supposed to be doing as communication was so poor. Not surprisingly, Celine, and most of the other students failed the course. Celine recalls returning to Bournville College a few years later. Appropriate communication support enabled her to participate more fully and she successfully obtained her first teaching certificate.

Green and Nickerson (1992) report that between 1983 and 1985, major national organisations, known as the Panel of Four, comprising members of the British Association for the Hard of Hearing (BAHOH), the British Deaf Association (BDA), the National Deaf Children's Society (NDCS) and the Royal National Institute for Deaf People (RNID), began to campaign for money to be made available for communication support for Deaf people. This was as a direct response from Deaf people themselves who were starting to become aware of their rights and demand a fairer access to education and training. Much of the campaigning focused on the MSC during its review of the provision for Deaf people in 1984.

In 1985 the Panel of Four established a working party to look at the needs of Deaf and hearing impaired YTS trainees (Simpson, 2007). It soon became apparent that the demand for communication support would far outstrip the supply. There were simply not enough Teachers of the Deaf (ToDs), or interpreters to fulfil the need. Those suitably qualified were already in employment. Also, it became apparent that some ToDs were not comfortable working in further education, because they had been trained to work in schools. Post compulsory education has a very different culture to compulsory education (schools) and some ToDs felt they were just not equipped to cope with the transition. Further discussion resulted in the realisation that a new role would need to be created, that of a communicator.

MSC were informed of the concerns, especially of the length of time it takes to train interpreters and, following a great deal of correspondence, MSC asked if there was any way in which it could help to alleviate the shortage of interpreters.

At this point, following discussions with Robin Caley as Chairman of the Council for the Advancement of Communication with Deaf People (CACDP), but also as Director of Birmingham Institute for the Deaf (BID), and Warren Nickerson, a lecturer with responsibility for Deaf students at

Bournville College of Further Education, Birmingham, CACDP submitted four possible schemes of training communicators/ interpreters to the MSC (Simpson, 2007). The training was to be funded as an Innovation Project. And so it was that the first MSC funded course to train Communicators to provide communication support to Deaf YTS trainees was born.

Chapter 2 gives an insight into this first training course, which commenced in September 1986, thanks to original course material provided by one of the first trainees, Nicola Richards. This chapter also includes details of the Derby Working Hands Project Certificate in Deafness Studies training course, which commenced in September 1987. Original course documentation was kindly provided by Chris Green, whose full report can be found in chapter 3.

It is worth noting that the funding for both the Birmingham and Derby courses were received at approximately the same time. Whilst the Birmingham course attracted MSC funding, the Derby course received funding from the EEC (European Economic Community) and Derbyshire County Council. Both streams of funding were for three year projects. However, whilst the Birmingham course sprang into action almost immediately, the first year of the Derby course, under the guidance of Chris Green, was spent on research, so training communicators did not commence until September 1987. Nickerson (1992) is very candid about the lack of preparation for the Birmingham course:

'Had we been required to provide a detailed course document of thirty to fifty pages, as is often the case when new courses are proposed in higher education, for example, this training scheme would never have commenced..... In the early stages many of us were working only a week ahead of the trainees......We believed that the opportunity might be lost if we did not seize it.... It would be wrong to convey an impression that the course lacked direction and planning. Certain areas were carefully constructed from the outset.' (Green and Nickerson, 1992, p121).

It is interesting to compare the content of the two training courses. Despite their differences, the outcome was the same. The role of the communicator had been debated and agreed over a considerable period of time, involving many meetings with members of NATED (National Association for Tertiary Education for Deaf People). A brief history is shown below. More details are shown in chapter 16.

Other notable developments which took place during the 1970s and early 1980s include:

NATED

In 1976 a small group of Teachers of the Deaf working as individuals in colleges, were invited by Peter Greenwood to meet in Bradford to share experiences and professional support. They started by collating examination arrangements for Deaf students. The group decided to hold a bigger, regional meeting to include more people and this took place in Sheffield in 1977. It led to a national meeting and the National Study Group in Further Education for the Hearing Impaired was established, with Joyce Sutton as the first Chair. The group became NATED in 1984, and founder members, besides Peter Greenwood and Joyce Sutton included Mike Hanson, Joe Pearce and John Hatton.

This group was responsible for all the early work with examination boards in negotiating examination arrangements. They promoted the need for clear communication and language modification and developed the 'Language of Examinations' booklet.

The Council for the Advancement of Communication with Deaf People (CACDP)

In 1976, the British Deaf Association submitted an application for the funding of a Communication Skills Project to the Department of Health and Social Security. It was a response to the Association's concern that sign language skills were declining at a time when Deaf people were becoming aware of the educational, economic and social opportunities available, so the need for sign language interpreting was increasing.

The three-year Communication Skills Project was approved and received £133,000, which at the time was one of the largest grants in support of Deaf people. Towards the end of this project there was a concern that the progress made would be halted or lost unless there was an organisation capable of continuing the work.

Following much discussion and numerous meetings, on 2 November 1980 CACDP was founded (Simpson, 2007, p42). At this time, CACDP's objectives were to:
1. Promote training in communication with Deaf people
2. Conduct a system of examinations in such skills
3. Maintain and administer a UK Register of interpreters
4. Encourage research and collate information relevant to the improvement of communication skills
5. Do all such other things as are incidental or conducive to the attainment of the above objects.

The organisation became independent in 1982. Success as CACDP drove the organisation to take stock and give a greater focus towards their vision of a society in which Deaf people have full access. The commitment to share knowledge and recognise skills in the languages and communication methods used by Deaf and Deafblind people led them to become Signature in January 2009 (Signature [online, n.d.]).

Deaf Rights Movement

The mid 1970s saw the rise of the Deaf Rights movement, including groups such as Britain's National Union of the Deaf (NUD) and the growth in the number of Deaf activists pressing for rights to sign language and Deaf identity.

One of the greatest examples was the mass 'Deaf President Now!' revolution at Gallaudet University, Washington USA in 1988 where the Deaf students and their Deaf and hearing supporters revolted against the university after the Governors had (again) elected a hearing President. The Governors eventually succumbed and elected King Jordan as their first ever Deaf president.

The status and recognition of British Sign Language (BSL) was given a major boost when in 1986, the late Diana, Princess of Wales became the patron of the British Deaf Association and subsequently demonstrated her skills in BSL at the BDA Centenary Congress in Brighton in 1990. There was a media frenzy and many people were inspired to learn the language.

The British Deaf Association

In 1971, at its congress in Bournemouth, the British Deaf and Dumb Association changed its name to the British Deaf Association (BDA). This was in time to meet the implementation of the Chronically Sick and Disabled Persons Act, 1970, which imposed statutory duties on local authorities to provide for the welfare of disabled people, including the Deaf, and encourage them to overcome their disabilities.

From this moment onwards, the BDA began to be more proactive in their approach to campaigning for the wider use and recognition of sign language (or British Sign Language as it had now become). Some notable achievements in the promotion of sign languages include the publication of the BSL/English dictionary, the success in getting official recognition of sign languages through the European Parliament in 1987, and most importantly the official recognition of British Sign Language in 2003 (BDA [online, n.d.]).

Clearly the 1970s and 1980s were times of great changes concerning communication support for Deaf people. This chapter has given an insight into some of these changes and outlined the need for training of communicators to be established.

The following chapter describes the content and structure of the first two formal training courses for communicators, which took place in Birmingham and Derby.

2
In The Beginning: Courses

The First MSC Funded Communicator Training Course 1986

The first training course specifically to train communicators to enable Deaf young students to take part in Youth Training Schemes (YTS) commenced in October 1986. It was funded by the Manpower Service Commission (MSC) and was an initiative between Birmingham Institute for the Deaf (BID) and Bournville College, Birmingham.

Due to the urgency at the time to train communicators in order to try to meet the increasing demand by young Deaf people to access training schemes, the decision was made to recruit candidates without necessarily any prior sign language skills. The belief was that by offering a full time training course with a large amount of sign language tuition, candidates would quickly become proficient in sign language.

Part of the conditions of the MSC funding was that candidates should be unemployed before commencing the training.

Green and Nickerson (1992) explained that it had already been decided to divide the training into two separate schemes. Apparently, not all candidates were expected to be able to reach the Stage 3 sign language level in such a short period of time. Also, some local people who had already achieved Stage 2 were keen to undertake what they perceived to be a Stage 3 crash course. Scheme 2 would only be allowed to proceed if the initial scheme, Scheme 1 was deemed to have been successful. Success would mainly be defined by the MSC in terms of skills acquisition.

It is fortuitous that Nicola Richards, one of the original trainees on the first communicator training course in Birmingham in 1986 is a secret hoarder. She kept all the material from the course and by sharing elements, enabled us to present an accurate picture of what the training entailed. The first timetable (the original copy is written in Warren Nickerson's handwriting) is reproduced here:

First MSC Funded Communicator Training Course Information

A COURSE IN:	Communicating with Deaf People
AT:	Bournville College of Further Education Bristol Road South BIRMINGHAM B31 2AJ
COURSE DATES:	Scheme 1. 6th October 1986 – 21st April 1987 Scheme 2. 22nd April 1987 – 24th July 1987 (For trainees who successfully complete Part 1 and who wish to develop additional sign language skills)
RECRUITMENT AREA:	National

1986/7 Timetable

Bournville College of Further Education	Birmingham Institute for the Deaf (BID)	Communicating with Deaf People		6 October 1986 – 17 April 1987	
MONDAY (BID)	Meeting the adult Deaf Community at the BID Focus: literacy	Discussion and Project Work at BID			
TUESDAY (BID)	Group Tutorial at BID	Introducing issues and organisations			
WEDNESDAY (COLLEGE)	Keyboard Skills S. Hiles	Language and learning difficulties in FE/ YTS and tutorials C. Reeves	British Sign Language C. Reeves		British Sign Language C. Reeves
THURSDAY (COLLEGE)	Keyboard Skills S. Hiles	English Language and Information Technology	Sociology C. Brooks	Private Study	Developmental Psychology H. Hughes
FRIDAY (COLLEGE)	Personal and Career development	English Language and Information Technology	British Sign Language C. Reeves		British Sign Language C. Reeves

PART 1: AIMS AND OBJECTIVES

A: To provide skills training in the various modes of communication used by Deaf people for hearing people wishing to work with Deaf people.

1. Developing an understanding of Deafness in terms of its personal and social effects, and its implication for personal growth and development, education and training.

2. Introducing British Sign Language – a language used by most pre-lingually profoundly Deaf people in this country.

3. Providing broad based and in depth skills training in the

use of sign language, lipspeaking, Deaf-blind communication, keyboard skills and information technology.

4. Involving trainees with Deaf people to develop an awareness of Deaf culture and to offer insight into difficulties encountered by Deaf people.

B: To assess trainees' skills through evaluation and validation to external national assessing agencies e.g. Council for the Advancement of Communication with Deaf People (CACDP)

C: To train people to a level of skills in communicating with Deaf people so as to be enable them to gain employment in areas such as social work assistants, residential care assistants, assistants in schools for Deaf children and YTS support work where communication skills, not teaching skills, are paramount.

D: To prepare successful trainees for additional intensive course in sign language communication.

PART 2: COURSE SYLLABUS

This course is intended to be 60% college based, 40% placement with Deaf people e.g. social services or voluntary agency.

This will be structured so as to provide an initial block period in college (to include a three day residential) followed by block placement and then assuming a pattern of three days in college, two days in placement. There will be a second three day residential at the end of the course.

A: Understanding Deafness and Deaf culture
1. Developmental
2. Medical
3. Psychological
4. Sociological
5. Organisational

B: Communication skills

1. Total communication philosophy
2. Non-oral communication
3. Communication and language development
4. British Sign Language
5. Lip speaking
6. Deaf/blind communication

C: English Language

1. Difficulties for Deaf people
2. Paraphrasing
3. Notetaking skills

D: Keyboard skills and basic computer operations

1. Computer keyboards
2. Electronic and electric typewriting

E: Information technology

1. Introduction
2. Uses of information technology with Deaf people
3. Special adaptations e.g. VISTEL (telephone for Deaf people)

F: Technical aid

1. Range available
2. Appropriate use
3. Care and maintenance

G: Video

1. Use of machine
2. Use of camera
3. Making own films including editing

Nicola, along with three other candidates, chose to leave the course after this initial Scheme 1 period, having successfully gained the Stage 2 qualification in sign language. She found work as a freelance Stage 2 communicator.

Four new candidates in-filled the vacant positions on Scheme 2 of the training course. The second scheme contained a higher percentage of sign language – almost 50% of the time – at this stage. Several of the candidates had made their intentions clear during the initial interview process. They were intent upon becoming interpreters. Green and Nickerson (1992) are very open in explaining that the infill situation was viewed by both candidates and course tutors as a fast way to acquire Stage 3. It is interesting to note that many of these initial candidates are still working in the field of Deaf education or interpreting, twenty five years after qualifying as communicators.

The Working Hands Project

The following information is taken from the original Working Hands Project course documentation which was kindly provided by Chris Green. Warren Nickerson admitted that rather than risk losing funding by spending valuable time developing a thirty to fifty page course document, the Birmingham communicator course was packaged very quickly. In contrast, it is worth noting that the Derby Working Hands Project Certificate in Deafness Studies course document is a very sturdy forty seven pages long. Those involved in developing this course decided to take time to plan thoroughly and produce a very professional looking (for its time) course document.

The Working Hands Project Certificate in Deafness Studies was a joint European Economic Community (EEC)/Derbyshire County Council initiative which was originally delivered as a two year part-time course, every Monday during college terms commencing October 1987 at Derbyshire College of Higher Education, Western Road, Mickleover, Derby. Chris Green was the Project Leader. The following information is extracted from the original course document, dated 1987:

1. Background

For many years a large proportion of profoundly Deaf people have been unable to participate in provision made available to the general public in the area of education, training and in-service staff development due to their restricted use of English language. When at school, the Deaf child has either the cushion of a sheltered environment or support from a special teacher in an ordinary school. Upon leaving school (or college in Derbyshire) and entering the adult world of work, the support usually stops until something goes wrong and a social worker is called in, often too late.

Learning does not cease at school leaving age. We are constantly learning about our environment, about our work, about other people's work, how to improve our standard of living, how to adapt and control our way of life. Profoundly Deaf people, who are effectively without hearing or speech, are unable to fully participate in equal opportunity programmes of education and training. The denial of access to these and other social freedoms is in effect to ignore their basic civil rights.

Derbyshire Social Services recognised the need to fill this gap in provision many years ago and put together proposals which culminated in the setting up of the Two-Can Project. This is primarily concerned with adult education for Deaf people. The next job was to find enough people with communication skills to carry on the learning process in the world of work – an outreach programme. Finding these people proved impossible. There are virtually no personnel with sufficient skills to act as communicators or to help with instructing Deaf people in this area. This is highlighted by using the YTS (Youth Training Scheme) as an example. In 1986 the MSC (Manpower Services Commission) put a sum of money aside (£350,000) to pay for CSD (Communication Support for the Deaf) but only a tiny proportion was spent because communicators were so difficult to find. The need for security of employment means that most people with sign language skills are already employed either as social workers with Deaf people, interpreters or as Teachers of the Deaf (ToDs). The areas of work of a communicator with Deaf people falls between these other professional roles.

2. Rationale

In 1985 Social Services put together another package of proposals to train twelve people to a good standard of communication so that they would form the basis of a pool of communicators to service the Derbyshire area. There were insufficient funds for Derbyshire to run the scheme alone, so in 1986 submissions were put to the EEC (European Economic Community). An agreement was made to share the funding of a three year project starting in December 1986 between EEC and Derbyshire Social Services. The Working Hands Project was born. A management committee was formed of members taken from the host College, Social Services and Derbyshire County Council.

During the first six months of this project, research was undertaken to establish the communication needs of profoundly Deaf people in the post school setting. Working with local Deaf people the Working Hands team has so far identified the following categories:

2.1 Industry and Commerce
Interviews and Induction Programmes:
Introductions and explanation of hierarchy
Geography of establishment
The working day, transport etc.

Pay and conditions:
Wage and Tax issues
Bonus

Rotas and Schedules
Disciplinary procedures and complaints
Tribunals
Union meetings
Job role
Redundancy / Retirement / Factory moves
Share Issues

Information dissemination:
Staff meetings
Staff awareness programmes
Health and Safety
Fire Drills / First Aid
In-Service training
Promotion boards, triennial reviews

Education and Training:

Leaving School:
Conferences
Careers advice
Visits and placements
YTS
Further/ Higher Education advice
Applications/ Interviews/ Induction
Student Union

Action for jobs:
Schemes such as CP, JTS, ITEC, NWS, ATP
   (see table of Acronyms)
Job Induction schemes
Applications
Interviews
Induction and support

Adult Education:
Evening classes
Personal development

Community Education

2.2 Information and Services

Central and local Government agencies:
DHSS (Department of Health and Social Security)
Job Centres
Job Clubs

Local issues:
Council issues
Housing
Education
MPs and Council surgeries
Political and Council meetings
Conference and debates / open meetings

Personal and social:
Hire purchase
Banking
Share issues
Para-medical (Opticians, Chiropodist)
Para-legal (house buying, insurance)
School visits
Childminders
Voluntary work
Societies and associations
Religious involvement
Women's rights / Ethnic groups

This is by no means exhaustive but nevertheless proves that things which are taken for granted by people with normal hearing can become major obstacles for those with a hearing problem. The grant for Working Hands from the EEC stipulates that the course should prepare students for employment. Since money is available to pay for communicators in the first two categories it is these areas that the course concentrates upon. There is the possibility, however, that in the future money may be made available for communication support for Deaf people in category 2.2.

Through practical experience in working with Deaf people, interviews with social workers, Teachers of the Deaf together with employers, trainers and the general public, the role of the 'Communicator/ Instructor' has been defined and the skills needed to fulfil this role have been established.

2.3 Present Provision

There are at present five centres offering initial 'Teacher of the Deaf' training in Great Britain. None of these centres offer training in working with Deaf adults and only one centre offers even basic sign language skills. All of these courses will cease when ACSET proposals submitted to the Secretary of State for Education in 1984 and outlined in the HMSO publication 'Better Schools' are implemented in 1989......

Communicator training is very much in its infancy. Only one course exists at present, sponsored by MSC and run at Birmingham Institute for the Deaf and Coventry Technical College. This course is endorsed by the Council for the Advancement of Communication with Deaf People (CACDP) and offers their Certificate in Communication with Deaf People Stage 2 (Intermediate). Another course is planned at the City Literacy Institute in London but funding arrangements have not yet been finalised.

2.4 Role of the Communicator/Instructor

Many of the areas described in 2.1 and 2.2 would become accessible to profoundly Deaf people if sign language communicators were made available. Other opportunities mentioned require direct or indirect instruction by trained personnel with specific vocational skills. Very few trainers have knowledge of the subject being taught and the skills necessary to transfer the knowledge to a Deaf client. To supply even a local Deaf population with the range of personnel using existing trainers requires the use of interpreters with some basic knowledge of the subject. Communicator/ Instructor is an amalgam of the two roles in order to provide a flexible response to the variety of tasks they will be required to perform, such as:

i.   An interpretation of spoken English to sign language, lip speaking/written notes

ii. An interpretation of sign language to spoken English language

iii. Instruction in problem solving and task analysis

iv. Intermediate instruction

v.   Explanation of English text

vi. Committing ideas into effective written English

vii. Awareness talks to 1) peers 2) employers 3) employees

viii. Advising/Counselling on background knowledge (accessing the system)

The style and level of input demanded of a communicator will depend on individual circumstances. Once the services are understood by the Deaf person, s/he will dictate the support approach in conjunction with employers, tutors and other concerned professionals. The amount of support may vary from an half-hour interview to an open-ended commitment for regular communication sessions. Under YTS regulations, for instance, a profoundly Deaf young person may have up to 500 paid hours of communication support over the two year scheme.

The role of the Communicator/Instructor therefore is to fill the central core of communication need which cannot be serviced by existing full time professionals such as social workers or teachers.

3. Aims of the Course

To train students to a level of competency so that on completion of the training they can be accepted for employment as Communicators and Instructors for Deaf people in vocational related situations.

The students will also be prepared for further self-motivated development in Deafness-related practices on completion of the course, such as Teacher of the Deaf or social worker with Deaf people or sign language interpreters.

1. Objectives

As Communicator/Instructors are a new concept in the public service field, examples of good practice and possible role models are difficult to find. However, Teachers of the Deaf, social workers and volunteers who have proved competent in the role of Communicators, together with tutors, trainers and management who have proven instructing abilities, have exhibited a variety of qualities which provide professional guidelines to adhere to. These objectives can be defined as:

1. An ability to adapt to the needs of the individual.
2. Fluency in British Sign Language and the ability to adapt to other communication modes such as lip speaking and Signs Supporting English.
3. Knowledge of the various roles of other professionals.
4. Good supervision skills – the ability to know when to intervene and when to withdraw.
5. Knowledge of the working environment.
6. Background knowledge of the subject matter to be interpreted. Preparation of appropriate materials and use and knowledge of available resources.
7. Good general communication skills (working with others). Sensitivity, diplomacy and tact. How, when and who to

refer difficulties to.

8. The ability to change English structure without losing content.

9. Consistency in style and approach.

10. Knowledge of Deaf culture and its implications (within a hearing world).

4. Scheme of Work

1. Duration and mode of attendance

The course will be 8 hours per week for 2 years during the normal college year of 36 weeks. There will also be a residential weekend at the beginning of each year. Two other days are set aside for conferences, visits and other aspects of distance learning, and will be arranged later. These 'floating days' will compensate for time lost due to Bank Holidays. The provisionally planned course day for 1987/88 will be Monday 9.00am to 5.00pm with an additional session of 1.5 hours of sign language. This additional session will depend upon the trainee's skill level at entry, and will be chosen from one of the following:

1. Sign language session based at the college

2. One evening session per week at a local Deaf Club

3. Video work

4. Directed study

In the second year the evening sessions will be flexible and arranged to suit the individual, as it will be a practical placement with a Deaf person. The course will start in October with a residential weekend.

The provisional timetable for the Working Hands Course is as follows:

4.2 Course timetable for year one:

Residential block 1	Immersion Weekend	Communication and Language			
9.00-10.00	11.00-12.30	1.30 - 3.00	3.30 - 5.00	+ 1.5 hrs	0.5 hrs
Term 1					
Sign Language	Behavioural Studies	Computing	Language & Comm.	Sign Language	
Term 2					
Sign Language	Deafness Studies	Computing	Language & Comm.	Sign Language	
Term 3					
Sign Language	Social Policy	Computing	Instruction Technology	Sign Language	
Floating day 1	Conference/ Visits				
Floating day 2	Conference/ Visits				

Residential block 2	Immersion Weekend	BSL			
9.00-10.00	11.00-12.30	1.30 - 3.00	3.30 - 5.00	+ 1.5 hrs	0.5 hrs
Term 1					
Sign Language	Social Policy	Sign Language	Computing	Placement	
Term 2					
Sign Language	Deafness Studies	Sign Language	Language & Comm.	Placement	
Term 3					
Sign Language	Personal Studies	Sign Language	Vocational enhancement	Placement	
Floating day 1	Conference/ Visits				
Floating day 2	Conference/ Visits				

4.3 Breakdown of study area:

Breakdown of course elements in hours (now known as Guided Learning Hours):

	UNIT	YEAR 1	Resid.	YEAR 2	Resid.	TOTAL
1	Sign Language	93	16	93	16	218
2	Behavioural Studies	13.5		–		13.5
3	Language & Communication	31.5		18		49.5
4	Computing	46.5		13.5		60
5	Deafness Studies	18		18		36
6	Social Policy	15		13.5		28.5
7	Instruction Techniques	15		–		15
8	Personal Studies	–		15		15
9	Vocational Enhancement	–		15		15
	Tutorials	15.5		15.5		31
	Placement	–		46.5		46.5
	Conferences/Meetings	16		16		32
	TOTAL HOURS	**280**		**280**		**560**

Glossary of Terms

ACSET	Advisory Committee on the Supply and Education of Teachers
ATP	Adult Training Programme
BSL	British Sign Language
CACDP	Council for the Advancement of Communication with Deaf People
CP	Community Programme
CSW	Communication Support Worker
DHSS	Department for Health and Social Security
EEC	European Economic Community
HMSO	Her Majesty's Stationery Office
ITeC	Information Technology Centre
JTS	Job Training Scheme
MPs	Members of Parliament

MSC   Manpower Services Commission
NWS   New Workers Scheme
YTS   Youth Training Scheme

3

In the Beginning: I Was There

Chris Green

Interview: Thursday 5 January 2012, Derby

Chris originally trained as a primary school teacher, working with eight and nine year olds, then started working with Deaf children at a Newcastle school (Northern Counties School for the Deaf). He taught progressively up the school years, or as Chris himself put it, the children just got older and older. He trained as a Teacher of the Deaf in Edinburgh at the time of Colville, Brennan and Lawson, all great luminaries. Later, he started teaching at a unit in Gateshead with school leavers, trying to get them into placements and colleges, which Chris claims, was difficult to say the least.

Chris then saw a job advertised in Derbyshire to work specifically with Deaf students in colleges of further education. He applied, was successful and went to Derbyshire to set up the service. There, he started talking to people who were doing similar work in school bases in the region. An organisation called NATED (The National Association for the Tertiary Education for Deaf People) kept cropping up in conversations. Subsequently, it was through going to NATED meetings and networking with various people that Chris's difficult task was made a little more possible.

The number of Deaf students in the colleges where Chris was working in Derbyshire was increasing all the time but Chris was working alone. He was beginning to struggle, so he had to look somewhere for a source of assistance. At the time there were various statutory schemes known by the following acronyms:

1. YTS. Youth Training Scheme, which was an on-the-job training course for school leavers aged 16 – 17, managed by the Manpower Services Commission.

2. WEEPs. Work Experience Programmes which were introduced by the Government in 1976 in an attempt to stem the growing tide of unemployment amongst the young. The 'WEEP' element of the programme referred to Work Experience on Employers' Premises, where 'trainees' received an allowance and there was a requirement that schemes should provide counselling and careers guidance as well as (if possible) training in social and life skills.

3. YOPs. The Youth Opportunities Programme which was a scheme for helping 16 to 18 year olds into employment, introduced in 1978 by James Callaghan's government, and which ran until 1983.

Deaf students were enrolling on these training schemes. However, after a little research, Chris realised that these schemes could also fund somebody as an assistant to help him, because the government literally paid employers to find jobs for young people at that time. Chris had an idea about where he could possibly find a suitable person to take on this work, so he went to the local sign language class, found somebody who was eligible for a YOP scheme, took him into college without any training, and put him to work with the Deaf students on computers. The name of the person was Lindsay Davies, also known as Mark Davies.

European Funding

At the same time as Chris was involved with NATED, he got to know people in the Social Services in Derby, who were supplying the interpreting support for Deaf students in colleges in Derby. Chris met Karen Gowing, who was very influential in expanding the interpreting service for education. They worked together on a proposal – Karen knew about possible European funding – and they submitted a three year scheme to develop training for people to work with Deaf students and trainees. Funding was readily available then, because it was the time of YOPs and WEEPs, and the YTS scheme was just being introduced. Chris and Karen put a course proposal together and won the funding they needed, which was massive (at the time) – about £180,000 over three years. They started with a year of research, then put a course together.

NATED meetings were an excellent networking opportunity, at a time when email, the internet and other modern technology that we now take so much for granted did not exist, and that's where Chris met Warren Nickerson. At the first NATED meeting Chris attended in York, there were about fifty people there, mainly Teachers of the Deaf, working at various schools and colleges. In that environment there was a lot of support for a new profession to work specifically in FE (further education) where the demand was so different to the demands in schools.

This was when Chris started working with Warren and others, initially discussing what should be included in a CSW training course and what should not. In retrospect, some of the things that were included in the first training courses in Chris's view clearly should not have been. For example, Chris was doing a masters degree in Communication Studies and Linguistics at the time, and those things found their way into the course. Some aspects of social work went into the mix too. Some of it was good, but trainers were teaching certain elements in too much detail. Or, in retrospect, if it was a longer course, they could have added them for depth and background. There was no interpreter training. Chris wasn't an interpreter, so there were no features of interpreting on the course, with the exception of when Peter Llewellyn-Jones attended as a visiting lecturer on occasions to talk about interpreting, or what interpreters do. Chris recalled that Peter was just brilliant, a fantastic signer and teacher, and still is.

Social Workers as Interpreters

There were few interpreters around because it was a very new profession. Some social workers were working as interpreters in education, but there was no initial friction as CSWs started to appear on the scene. It seemed that the social workers were glad to give up the education side of things if they possibly could. But they had the skills in sign language and Chris and his team did not. Interpreting wasn't always required though, because more than half of the Deaf students were not sign language users but relied on their hearing aids. It was a case of give and take. The social workers, or interpreters, sometimes had to travel from Derby to Chesterfield, which took an hour in the traffic, typically to interpret a tutorial and then drive back again. It was madness, so it was clear that Chris needed to expand the service and have specialists on the spot.

Working Hands Project

After a year of research, Chris had written one of the first CSW training courses, which was known as 'The Working Hands Project Certificate in Deafness Studies.' This was designed as a two year, part-time course, consisting of one day per week in college. The course was due to start during the second year of the three year project, in September 1987, so Chris needed to recruit trainees. The conditions of the funding were that trainees must be unemployed people. Other conditions stated there had to be a mixture of genders, something like seven men and fifteen women, a certain number of the men had to be over 25, some of the women had to be under 18. Chris's memory is hazy, but the funding providers were very specific about who could be recruited and who could not. Chris advertised locally and visited the Deaf Clubs and press-ganged people who were interested in working with Deaf people. Some candidates were working in shops; one had come from Boots the Chemist and had to give up her job to go on the course. Quite a few people had learnt a bit of sign language, or had relatives who were Deaf or partially Deaf, and they wanted to do more, so gave up their jobs to join the course. This was the only course of its type in the area.

It became clear however, that one day per week training was not enough, so a one year full-time course was developed, starting in 1988. The second year of the part-time course was run in conjunction with the one year full-time course, so part-time Certificate in Deafness Studies students were studying alongside full-time students that year.

Chris and Warren were doing all the writing for the CSW course, but it wasn't a nationally recognised qualification, it was only a college certificate course. However, it was becoming more nationally recognised. Later, when BTEC/Edexcel were involved, candidates who had successfully achieved the Certificate in Deafness Studies from Derbyshire College of Higher Education had to do a 'top-up' of about thirty hours, in order to reach the national standard and thereby eventually qualify for the full CSW certificate.

After the success of the Derby, Bournville and Coventry training courses, other institutions were jumping on board, through NATED. Manchester College started to offer CSW training, with Rachel O'Neill (now working in Scotland), and also City Lit in London. After a few years it felt as though they were beginning to 'sing from the same hymn sheet'. By then it was mutually agreed what was useful and what wasn't in terms of course content; what they could reasonably include in that time and what they could not.

Funding was readily available throughout the period that Chris was involved. He decided to apply to various national examination boards in an attempt to get national recognition for the training. However, there was a problem – because the course was only certified by a college, the students were not eligible for funding in their own right. Chris therefore submitted the course documents to various national examination boards, including City & Guilds, RSA (Royal Society of Arts), BTEC (which later became Edexcel) etc. He knocked on various doors and explained about the new course and that he wanted recognition nationally. BTEC/Edexcel responded and agreed to accredit the course. This meant that students could get funding to go on the course wherever it was, so they were not limited to Derby. The process of getting the course recognised nationally involved a great deal of work. But the hard work paid off because when it was accepted by BTEC/ Edexcel, more colleges were happy to run the course because the students could get funding for themselves. Therefore, with sponsorship initially through European or MSC (Manpower

Services Commission) funding, individual students were able to obtain funding through local education authorities.

Recruiting candidates to the Deafness Studies course was no problem, especially when it became certificated and recognised as such. With the correct documentation, applications to offer the course could be submitted to academic boards at colleges and universities. It wasn't difficult to get funding and permission to run courses, but initially the assessments were the sticking point because of the standards; for example, how candidates' evidence was to be matched against the criteria for a pass and not pass. However once that was documented, it was quite easy to get it through academic boards to become certificated.

The Rise of the Communicator

The book written by Chris and Warren Nickerson, 'The Rise of the Communicator', was just meant to be a record of what Chris, Warren and their teams had achieved. It was a 'Vanity Press' venture, where authors funded publication themselves. No commercial publishers were interested in the book. The eventual publisher, Moonshine, was Chris's first student – Lindsay Davies, who went into publishing briefly, just for that one book! No profit was made on it because that didn't seem important to Chris and Warren at the time.

The idea for the book came about at a NATED meeting. Chris, Warren Nickerson and colleagues agreed that there needed to be a record of what had been achieved, before it was forgotten and lost. They had a couple of short meetings after the initial course in Birmingham and the Derby course had started. Students on the first course at Bournville/BID had completed their initial training in 1987 and twelve newly-qualified 'Communicators' had entered the workforce. During the second year, 1987-88, the course had moved from Bournville to Coventry. After one NATED meeting Chris and Warren discussed what to include in the book. Warren commented, 'Well, we must put in the Bournville/Coventry course because we have sponsorship for that, so it must be included in its entirety.' Eventually, Warren included details on every student on that first course. Chris and Warren took a week's leave and went to Center Parcs with an Apple Mac (an early version of the computer series). Their daily routine consisted of jogging in the morning, then writing something; going for a swim; then writing some more; having a glass of wine; then writing the rubbish bits! That's how the book came about. They tried to find a publisher, but nobody was interested so they asked Lindsay to publish it. They printed around two hundred copies which included a reprint. Forest Books (the specialist bookshop for Deaf related works) contacted Chris some years later and asked whether they would be reprinting the book. However, Chris and Warren weren't interested in reprinting because the book was meant to be just a record of what they had done.

A Seminal Volume

During our interview, we were surprised at Chris's playing down of the book, so we reminded him that it is such a seminal volume. All CSW course tutors tell their students that they must beg, borrow or steal a copy, and it is quoted all over the place, even though it is now twenty years since it was published, but Chris was very self–effacing. He said that Forest Books sold it for a while, for £15 or so, and that he and Warren received £5 each for each copy, which just about covered the costs involved. The book was simply a record of what they had done and was never intended to be a training manual.

Chris talked about ASLI (The Association of Sign Language

Interpreters), and mentioned that Peter Llewellyn-Jones is known to have been instrumental in forming this in 1987. The first item on the agenda in ASLI's first annual general meeting was 'Communicators'. We commented that we would be asking Peter about that when we came to interview him later. We asked Chris to explain some of the feelings around at that time, and he threw his head back, laughed and said, 'We were misunderstood!' Then he went on to explain that there was a lot of negativity due to several issues;

CSWs had to be unemployed when they started the training;

There was no minimum sign language at entry;

CSWs were not as skilled in sign language as interpreters;

CSWs didn't have interpreting training.

Interpreters Few and Far Between

It was true that CSWs were going into class with Deaf students and they were 'interpreting', or at least explaining the meaning of new vocabulary using sign-language, purely because there was nobody else to do that at the time. There were no interpreters in the room – interpreters were few and far between. Social workers, who had previously been doing the job of a CSW wanted to go back to being social workers. There were only CSWs there, available and willing to do a variety of tasks: transcribing videos, tutorials, lipspeaking and notetaking. Also they had some signing skills, so they did some interpreting, rightly or wrongly. Chris admitted that for the most part, with exceptions, they were doing it wrongly, but they were there. One other important issue, according to Chris, was that they were doing it 'on the cheap' compared to interpreters, although Chris never heard that voiced. Nobody ever said to him 'You're taking our jobs because you're doing it cheap.' But comments were made like 'Interpreters only work for 40 minutes, but there's a CSW going in for an hour and a half in a high-powered lecture'. In Chris's view, at that time, having a CSW in the classroom was better than a Deaf person sitting there understanding nothing. But nobody ever, in any meetings Chris attended, sat face-to-face with him and said 'What you are doing is wrong.'

Chris achieved BSL Stage 3 but he just didn't have the time to do the training that was needed to become an interpreter. He mused that being an interpreter has always been romantic, the top of the profession. But his skills were elsewhere. He would have loved to be an interpreter, but the practicality was that he couldn't be there for the 10% of the Deaf students who were sign language users, but he could be very useful by using other skills such as transcribing videos, indirect support, in the background. He could sit and talk one-to-one with a Deaf student using his BSL Stage 3 skills, but couldn't do the interpreting process part. Then there were the other 80 or 90% to consider, the biggest group of Deaf students who had other needs that didn't include interpreting. A lot of CSWs were in the same position.

Change of Job

One day Chris received a phone call from Stewart Simpson, Chief Executive of CACDP (The Council for Advancement of Communication with Deaf People), who said that he was interested to learn more about what Chris was doing and would like to visit to see for himself what a CSW did. Chris agreed and said 'Come any time you like'. Soon afterwards, Stewart Simpson and Ruth Roberts arrived one morning in the foyer of the college and sat in class, observing, for a full day of CSW training. About three weeks later Chris was offered a job with CACDP. He had not realised that Stewart Simpson's 'visit' had really been an interview! Chris accepted the offer and started working from home, travelling to Durham and London where he worked closely with Ruth for six years at CACDP on examinations as Director of Standards. Chris believes his appointment was for two reasons. The first was because of his experience writing exams for City & Guilds, BTEC, writing the CSW course and developing continual assessments and portfolios of evidence. These were just starting to be recognised as a way of presenting evidence and CACDP wanted to take advantage of this. The other reason was that, Chris believed, CACDP wanted to take the CSW training into their portfolio of qualifications.

Early CSW Registration Thoughts

Most of the time at CACDP, Chris was rewriting assessment procedures for BSL Stages 1, 2 and 3 and initiating Annual Standardisation Meetings. He really enjoyed his first few years at CACDP. It was wonderful and he worked with some brilliant people, but still kept his CSW hat on. He couldn't bear trying to get the CSW course into CACDP's portfolio because he had spent so long negotiating with BTEC/Edexcel, but he made sure that the parts of the CSW course that he felt should be with CACDP remained with them. Sadly the situation became very complicated with the new NVQs (National Vocational Qualifications). Ruth Roberts became the NVQ Development Officer, and around that time (1997), there was discussion and a start was made toward registration for CSWs. However, Chris's recollection was that they eventually decided that the Edexcel qualification was the registration – meaning that if someone had a CSW certificate, they were recognised as a qualified CSW. Edexcel was deemed to be the register for CSWs. If someone wanted a CSW, they could check if a person was qualified through Edexcel. But there was also discussion and debate about interpreters. There was a lot of falling out about interpreter registration because there were no interpreter standards at the time. People were arguing about which university degree was the best. Interpreters had no national qualification, but there was one for CSWs. Many people don't realise that – CSWs were there first.

Where Are You Now?

After leaving CACDP, Chris worked for ten years on the biggest children's interactive website in the world, as editor of GridClub, later to become SuperClubPlus. Funded by Channel 4 television and the Department for Education and Skills (DfES), it involved children from all over the world getting together on something akin to Facebook. The website was in thousands of schools in England, Scotland and Northern Ireland. The schools registered every child and then they could talk safely to children all over the world. Chris trained and examined moderators who analysed children's behaviour and kept them safe online. He even travelled to Australia on several occasions to establish the website and train staff. But eventually funding collapsed – in Chris's view schools were required to prioritise their spending and many decided to buy new carpets or white boards instead of teaching children how to be safe online. In 2008 Chris was made redundant. He worked for a charity called Village Aid for a year, which does work with children in Africa. He was also doing drama in schools, bringing to schools what rural life was like in Africa. Since then he has done bits and bobs – looked after chickens and an allotment. Although now a retired granddad and over 60, he still loves rock climbing. He lives in Bakewell with his wife, on a hill with his chickens. He still maintains that helping to 'invent'

CSWs is the most important thing he ever did, despite recently appearing at the Buxton Opera House as the professor in The Lion, The Witch and The Wardrobe.

In the Beginning: I Was There

Nicola Richards

A student on the first CSW course, in 1986.
Interview: Thursday 5th January 2012, Derby

Nicola completed a degree in 3D Ceramics (BA Hons) in Wolverhampton in 1982, then moved to Warwick to set up a workshop to make and sell ceramics.

During her degree she had a placement in a Primary school for two weeks. She was generally helping out but also teaching Art and Pottery lessons. There were three Deaf children in the class who communicated using British Sign Language (BSL) and they fascinated Nicola. When Nicola demonstrated making coil pots, the Deaf children were the only ones who 'got it' first time round and needed no further instruction (unlike the rest of the hearing children). Nicola also had a session with these three Deaf children where they all communicated entirely using drawings. Nicola felt disadvantaged as she was the one who could not sign. This placement triggered the subject matter for Nicola's thesis, investigating whether art and creativity could be a valuable means of developing learning, self-expression or communication and whether it could promote self-esteem and empowerment. Coincidentally it was around this time that Nicola started to wear a hearing aid, after suspecting a hearing loss for many years.

Whilst 'potting' Nicola started to learn sign language at her local college. The course was run by a local mother who had a Deaf son. This was before the British Sign Language Training

Agency (BSLTA) trained Deaf tutors. The sign language class consisted of signed phrases such as 'The quick brown fox jumped over the lazy dog'.

Interview for CSW Course

Nicola decided that she wanted to use sign language, so she met with Karen Hope who was then the Director of Warwickshire Social Services for Deaf People. Karen directed Nicola to the new pilot course for Communicators with Deaf People which Karen's partner, Warren Nickerson, was due to start delivering. Nicola went for an interview the following day and started the full time course the subsequent Monday, in September 1986. Little did Nicola realise what a momentous decision this was and how she would feature in the history of CSWs as being one of the very first qualified CSWs in the UK.

Nicola had not had any previous experience of sign language or Deafness, apart from meeting the three Deaf children during her work experience placement and her sign language tutor's son – and of course her own experience of hearing loss.

The pilot course that Nicola attended was called 'Communicating With Deaf People' and ran from Sept 1986–April 1987 on a full time basis. Candidates had to attend Bournville College of Further Education (Birmingham) for three days per week, then Birmingham Institute for the Deaf (BID) two days per week. Nicola then did a 'top up' course once the programme had been validated by BTEC (Business and Technology Education Council) during the years 1991-1994.

At the time there were no entry requirements for the course, apart from needing to be unemployed. The role of the CSW did not exist although the need for people to fill such a role had been identified as more and more Deaf young people and adults wanted to enter further education.

Luckily Nicola kept all her papers and notes from the original training course, so was able to give an accurate picture of how the course was structured and who taught on it. From the timetable opposite (in Warren Nickerson's own handwriting) the content of the pilot course for the new CSWs was as follows:

At Birmingham Institute for the Deaf (BID)

Mondays:

Adult job club and tutoring group – helping out, good practice for communication skills.

Deaf Social Workers would tell stories – this was excellent for practising receptive skills

Experiences from the Deaf Community were discussed.

Tuesdays:

Introducing issues and organisations; tutorials

Discussion and project work

At Bournville College:

Wednesdays:

Keyboard Skills

Language and learning difficulties for Deaf people in Further Education/ Youth Training Schemes (YTS)

BSL lessons from 1.15 – 4.30, starting at Level 1 through to Level 2 (others continued to Level 3 from April – June)

Thursdays:

English Language and Information Technology

Sociology

Developmental Psychology

Fridays:

Personal Career Development

1.15 – 4.30 BSL

COMMUNICATING WITH DEAF PEOPLE

6th Oct. 1986 – 17th April 1987

at Birmingham Institute for the Deaf — at Bournville College of F.E.

MONDAY — Meeting at the Birmingham adult deaf community Institute focus: literacy

TUESDAY — Group at Introducing and organisations / TUTORIAL B.I.D. issues / Discussion Project at B.I.D.

WEDNESDAY — DS72 KEY BOARD SKILLS S. Hiles / LANG + LEARN DIFFICULTIES IN F.E./YTS + TUTORIALS C. REEVES A406 / BRITISH SIGN LANGUAGE C. REEVES A406

THURSDAY — DS72 " / A406 ENGLAND + INFO TECH / A406 SOC. E. BROOKES / PRIVATE tons A406 / DEVELOPMENTAL PSYCHOLOGY A406 M. HUGHES

FRIDAY — A406 PERSONAL & CAREER DEVELOPMENT / " / BRITISH SIGN LANGUAGE A406

In 1987, candidates took the Deafblind Level 1 assessment (now equivalent to Level 2 as it included Communication: a seven minute conversation, and Guiding skills) and also a Clear Speech and Lipspeaking Assessment which was taught by

Glenda Bateman.

- Language Modification and Notetaking Skills were taught by Warren Nickerson (Teacher of the Deaf)
- Audiology and types of Deafness were also taught by Warren Nickerson, as was The Language of Examinations
- Information and Technology included adaptions and telephones, radio aids etc.
- The Code of Practice: BDA and Police & Criminal Evidence Act 1984.
- Project on Organisation: NATED, BATOD, RNID, Coventry Deaf Club, Social Services, Probation Service, FYD, Wycliffe House, Birmingham (mental health)

There was a visiting speaker from the Probation Service for Deaf People and a lot of input from Deaf people at BID and Christine Reeves for two afternoons each week.

The course was total immersion, full time, both at Bournville College and BID. Some students were living away from home so they all used to meet outside the course socially, usually at the Birmingham Deaf Club. Nicola did voluntary work at the Deaf Club with 'At Risk' children. She remembers meeting lots of Deaf people and being nervous about the first few visits to the Deaf Club.

Post-Training

Following the training, Nicola worked with Deaf adults funded by the Youth Training Scheme (YTS) and Manpower Services Commission (MSC), either learning skills or looking for employment. She supported Deaf students at Bournville College on a self-employed basis and recalls that she travelled to Birmingham, Sandwell, Handsworth etc for work.

She now realises that the first CSWs were a new breed. They

had to deliver a lot of Deaf Awareness to make others aware of the barriers that Deaf people faced and of the role of the CSW. Nicola liked the variety of the work involved.

Additional assignments included:
- **Deaf People in the Community Module**
  Equal Access and Opportunity
  The Children's Act 1989
  Report on a visit to an educational establishment
  Micro teaching – Deaf Awareness
  Essay – Deaf People in the Community
  Essay – Disability: A Social Condition – discuss
  Oral communication
- **Communication Skills Module**
  BSL 3 (required)
  Log book of support work completed (100 hours)
- **Language and Communication Module**
  BSL essay on aspect of BSL structure

Trainers on Nicola's course:
- Warren Nickerson (Lecturer at Bournville College): *Deafness issues and organisations, Further Education Institutions and how they function*
- Robin Caley (Director of BID): *Deaf Community, Deafness Issues, Job Club, Literacy Club at BID*
- Christine Reeves (Lecturer at Bournville College): *BSL Tutor Levels 1, 2 and 3*
- Karl Channing and Roger Sutton (Deaf Social Workers): *Story tellers for receptive skills*
- Clive Brooks (Bournville College): *Sociology*
- Margaret Hughes: *Developmental Psychology*
- Glenda Bateman (British Association of the Hard of Hearing: BAHOH): *Clear Speech Tutor and*

Assessor

- Sheila Grew (Principal Regional Officer of RNID): *Deafblind Trainer Level 1*
- Doug Alker: *Deafblind training*
- Graham Hicks: *Deafblind assessor*

Still in Contact With Any Students?

One student Nicola worked with for many years at City College Coventry is now not working due to ill health. Nicola is still in contact with two other students she supported, via Facebook and email. One is now the Head of the Wolverhampton University Interpreting Service and Nicola used to meet her occasionally via CHESS (Consortium of Higher Education Support Services) meetings.

The Difference Between CSWs Then and Now

Nicola feels that CSWs should receive training on interpreting skills, awareness of technology and audiology and support strategy skills. She also strongly believes that CSWs should keep themselves updated in professional matters and Deafness issues. Being a CSW in education, Nicola feels, is different from working as a community interpreter although sometimes a CSW may well be interpreting information to a BSL user. It entirely depends on the level of the course, the way that it is delivered, the level of BSL skills of the Deaf student, and the preferred mode of communication used by the Deaf person. At other times the job may entail filling in the gaps, altering the language register, notetaking, repeating information, facilitating communication between any hearing person and the Deaf student, assisting with research, assignment planning and writing.

Where Are You Now?

Twenty five years after completing that first training course at Bournville College, Nicola is still working in education with Deaf students. She worked for a number of years as a freelance CSW and then at Coventry Technical College before moving to Warwickshire College in 2006 where she is now a Tutor for Deaf Students. This job entails assessing Deaf learners, teaching literacy and numeracy to Deaf learners with additional needs, delivering cross-college Deaf awareness and supporting Deaf learners as a CSW. Nicola is also a committee member of NATED.

In the Beginning: I Was There

Tracey Kelsall

Interview: Thursday 5 January 2012, Derby

We met Tracey in a room at Derby College in the first week back after the New Year 2012. It was a windy day outside as we talked into the early evening. We asked Tracey when her first contact with Deaf people was. The answer was, way back when she was fifteen and still at school. The Royal School for the Deaf in Derby was keen to promote links with local schools so a group of Deaf pupils and hearing pupils went to France for a fortnight. The hearing pupils learnt very basic sign language in preparation for the trip. Each was paired up with a Deaf pupil (Tracey is still friends with her partner now) and they were let loose in France! She recalls that the hearing pupils were hopeless at French, but the Deaf pupils were brilliant at communicating with everybody. She says, "If we wanted to buy anything, we would take our Deaf friend with us and tell them to say 'I want that as cheap as possible' and get it!"

Horse Accident

Tracey left school and did other things – she loved horses so she worked at 'Riding for the Disabled' in Coventry. One day a couple of Deaf young boys arrived and she couldn't communicate with them. With only basic fingerspelling and a bit of sign language she found it difficult to teach riding 'because Deaf children need to let go of the reins to talk and the horses then gallop off across the field'. Unfortunately Tracey subsequently suffered an accident at the stables, which left her with a bad back injury, so she returned home to Derby, unemployed. Tracey was interested in doing some voluntary work. She met somebody who worked in the local Social Services who mentioned that there was a sign language course about to start and suggested she join. Tracey duly started a Stage 1 British Sign Language course. She must have been a natural, because on the second or third week her tutor announced, "Oh, you'll make an interpreter, you will." But back then, no-one knew what an interpreter was. Later, after she had achieved Stage 1 BSL she was introduced to Chris Green who was looking for people to join the 'Working Hands Project' which was one of the first CSW training courses. Tracey was asked to sign a piece of paper and attend a meeting. She was elated because she felt that was what she really wanted to do – like many others she had become addicted to sign language. Tracey was duly selected and started on the Working Hands Project Certificate in Deafness Studies course in September 1987, one day per week on a Monday.

Jumped From Stage 1 to Stage 3

At the beginning of the course there was not a lot of sign language training because many of the students had already achieved Stage 1 BSL before the start of the course. Tracey went straight from there to BSL Stage 3, which was possible at that time.

By October Tracey was working for the training group with Chris Green and Mary Walters of Communication Unlimited, a Derby based Communications/Interpreter Agency. Right from the start she was supporting Deaf students on the days that she wasn't on the course. It was very much a matter of learning on the job. If some difficulty happened while Tracey was working, she talked the problem through with the other students on the course. She remembers discussions starting with, 'Oops, such-and-such has happened! What do I do? Where do I go? How do I solve it?'. Tracey describes the experience as immersive, fascinating, on-the-job training. The Deaf students Tracey worked with had never been to higher education before, had no experience so didn't know what they wanted. It was a collaboration to find out. A lot of experimentation took place to try this and that, and if it didn't work, they had a cup of coffee and said 'should we try something else?'. If something didn't succeed, Chris Green had a look to see if he could do anything or make any suggestions. Tracey became skilled at liaising with the lecturers to find out the essential meaning of what they were delivering to the Deaf students. Most of the lecturers had no idea about how to include Deaf students either. Everything was an unknown quantity. It was new and exciting and addictive.

No One Knew What They Were Doing

Tracey recalled with a wry smile that nobody really knew what they were doing – everything was new. No one was qualified, but they were on the programme, so that was their defence. They were learning, so they were allowed to make mistakes, which in many ways was wonderful because at that time, experimenting was the best way to learn and people weren't afraid to make slip-ups. Then, the struggles and the solutions were incorporated into the course and shared with other students – not only on a local basis, but nationally also, through NATED (The National Association for Tertiary Education for Deaf People) and other associations. Sometimes there were 'eureka' moments, when people said 'I've found just the way of getting round that problem we have been discussing

– go and try it and let me know if it works.' The students were developing the training themselves.

Tracey recalls there were about eighteen students on the course to start with. There were quite a few dropouts because people needed to be unemployed to join the course, and there were restrictions to do with age and other issues. Also, some people thought that they wanted to work with Deaf people, but when they started they realised that it wasn't for them. Twelve students completed the initial two-year long, part-time course.

At the end of the course, when Tracey qualified, she continued working in education within the Support Service being set up with Chris at the Derbyshire College of Higher Education (which later became the University of Derby). During the time Tracey was studying on the Working Hands Project there was only one Deaf student at the college, but because they were succeeding, news got around and suddenly two more enrolled. Later, students came from all over the country, they even had a Deaf student from Beirut! In the end they were working through five different spoken languages, not only sign language.

Engineering and Pure Maths

Tracey was working as a CSW supporting a Deaf student in engineering and pure maths in the evening, which she remembers was heaven because she was the only female in the room! Everybody took the mickey out of her, including the Deaf student. It was good because it meant that the Deaf student became one of them, against her! It was natural integration, and it worked! It made a lot of difference to the Deaf student because he got to know the other students socially too. Many of the CSWs viewed the work holistically – it wasn't a 9-5 job, it was more than that, so Tracey was willing to work during coffee breaks and go to the bar afterwards to interpret. Then, gradually the hearing peers started to learn sign language, so she could go home early. The friendship forged between Tracey and that Deaf student continues today.

The tutors on the Working Hands programme were very keen that the students had links with the local Deaf community, and for their part, the local Deaf people felt it was really important to train the students to do what that they wanted. They were actually very proud of the students. Deaf people started to attend public meetings, and then - lo and behold - a CSW was at the front signing and doing their best. The Deaf people were pleased because this had never happened before. The collaboration was not only in education, it was in the community too. This was simply because there were no interpreters about at that time. The only people who could interpret were social workers, who were keen to develop interpreters in other professions so that they could do what they had trained to do – work as social workers. At that time there was no ASLI (Association of Sign Language Interpreters) and no interpreter training - there was nothing. Things were starting to develop with interpreting at the same time as communication support work.

International Influence

When the Working Hands Project finished, many people in the team that were training became the local communications agency called 'Communication Unlimited'. Their aim was to develop services in education locally within the university but also through NATED, working with further education departments and schools nationally. Indeed, their influence was international because they received funding for a research trip to America, visiting Rochester, New York and Hartford,

Connecticut (the first American School for the Deaf) and developed links. People from America came to Derby to see what the team were doing there. Staff from British universities suddenly discovered that Deaf students had enrolled and had no idea what to do to support them, so they called Tracey and her team. Visitors were welcomed to talk about any issues surrounding supporting Deaf students in education. There was a collective sharing of ideas and expertise and contacts at the time.

We asked Tracey what other training she undertook and she replied that, in the early years, there was hardly any training out there. People were taking whatever training they could find. Tracey was recommended to jump from BSL Stage 1 to BSL Stage 3. Although there was a BSL Stage 3 course in Derby, she made the unusual decision to go to Scotland to train because she didn't want to learn only regional signs, she wanted to broaden her experiences. She was told (in the BSL Stage 3 exam) to get herself on another course. The only training available at the time was a two year pilot course at Bristol University. Later, she ended up as a student on a pilot course for one of the first interpreter training assessments. None of the students were given a certificate at the end of the Bristol University course because the university realised that they hadn't actually planned the course properly in relation to the examination. They assessed the candidates on material that they hadn't trained them for.

Around this time, Peter Llewellyn-Jones was just setting up the interpreting course at Wolverhampton, so Tracey was one of his first students there. She had to attend on a part-time basis because there were lots of Deaf students at Derby University – she was determined not to give up what was developing in Derby. Tracey completed the course and was very proud because she achieved a 1st class BA Honours degree.

Attending the interpreting course helped Tracey to see things from a different perspective; there were a lot of CSWs at the time turning their back on their CSW qualification, almost denying they even had one, possibly because of criticism from interpreters. However, Tracey has always held the view that CSWs should train in many different ways to enhance their CSW work, because education is a specialism in her view. People wanted to go on to work in law, as legal interpreters or medical interpreters etc., but Tracey thought, 'Great, but what about education?' She recalls feeling that if people didn't know the 'rules of the game', they couldn't survive within education. Sometimes, co-working CSWs had to be 'good cop, bad cop', to properly support the Deaf students to get what they required. There were lots of things that CSWs did in education that they couldn't do in other domains because it wouldn't be appropriate, and vice versa. Education is very much based on teamwork. It's the team that makes or breaks it. Sometimes Tracey admits that she was not the best person to be in a particular classroom. A CSW may be professional, qualified, have the appropriate skills, knowledge and experience, but the chemistry might not work with that lecturer. That might be absolutely destroying the communication and the student cannot access the information. But the good thing about it is that you can always go back to your team and say 'Right, I know this isn't working – you go in, you try, you work with him.' Tracey thinks that, with education we are not frightened to do things like pick a pen up or explain things in different ways.

Interpreters Blinkered Toward the Education Role

Tracey thinks that interpreters – the pure interpreters, those that have gone through the route of the degree only – become slightly blinkered to what the role in education actually is. Tracey claims that she's not saying that you don't need to be the best bilingual worker that you can be, if that is what that student requires. But also you need to be a good bilingual worker because you are working with hearing people too. You need to be able to explain exactly what that particular Deaf person needs and there are ways of doing it and not doing it. When you work in education, you've got to work with that person every day for three years. If someone works as a free-lance interpreter and does a meeting for two hours, if they upset somebody, they don't have to take a job with them again. If you work in education, you've got to park your car next to that person and have coffee with them and get on with them. Tracey thinks that your skills and your way of dealing with them is completely different when you're a pure interpreter compared to a bilingual person who is working as a CSW in education.

Tracey feels lucky that her specialist area was bilingual work. A lot of the students she worked with were BSL users that other CSWs couldn't understand – the more challenging signers. Tracey revelled in it, but kept her feet firmly on the ground. She was also able to teach on the CSW courses and become a mentor, encouraging people and fostering them. She encouraged students to shadow her, and then had them share sessions in the classroom. Everyone supported as many people as possible.

When Chris Green left to go to CACDP (Council for the Advancement of Communication with Deaf People, now known as Signature), everything changed. A new head of the unit arrived who had a different emphasis and was not supportive of what the team were doing, and the unit became part of Student Support. The new head didn't want the team to teach CSWs, even though they explained that some of the

CSW students were recruited to join the working team because they fitted in with the ethos of developing support with Deaf students. The new boss wanted to stop that altogether. It was such a shame because just before Chris left they developed the Notetaker Training Programme which then became a qualification with CACDP; the team went on to train trainers to deliver that programme; Tracey became an external verifier for CACDP to try to maintain standards; the college became a Centre of Excellence; notetakers were being trained, then used both in the university and in the local area.

The new head was unmoved and insisted it should all stop. So, when Tracey was asked to work for Derby College for Deaf People (DCDP) at the Royal School for the Deaf she couldn't get there fast enough! She headed up a support service at a college in Chesterfield for a year, then went into Wilmorton College to develop services there with a large team of CSWs and trainees. Eventually Tracey ended up inheriting the CSW course and training CSWs at Derby College for Deaf people. Sadly the college then lost its funding and was forced to close. All staff were made redundant. It was the last straw and Tracey felt burnt out – she had had enough. She had been involved in trying to develop CSWs nationally; on the NATED committee; on the CACDP committee; travelling doing notetaking; training the trainers; an external verifier on interpreting; involved in training and trying to do everything. She realised she couldn't do any more and needed a real break, so went off to work for her husband, who has a transport business. Tracey won her HGV (Heavy Goods Vehicle) license and started driving lorries.

Where Are You Now?

Tracey is still working in education as a CSW because recently, someone from Derby University phoned her and said,

'Come back, your skills are wasted there, get back here.' They realised that they didn't have anyone on their team who could support a student on a high level course, so they thought of Tracey because she had trained on the CSW programme with them. So now she works a few days a week at the University of Derby supporting Deaf students in computing, engineering and architecture. She is very happy to stay in education.

Tracey mused that they had worked very hard at the beginning to set things up - it was a creative time where there was so much going on and huge advances. She has watched people develop, who started in an unassuming way on CSW courses and who are now in positions of influence, making things happen for Deaf students. She believes that the ethos that was put into the original courses is still there and going strong.

In the Beginning: I Was There

Sean and Karen Nicholson

Interview: Wednesday 26 October 2011, Lytham St Anne's.

Sean and Karen started the CSW course in the same year, but in different cohorts. The course was jointly organised by the Birmingham Institute for the Deaf (BID) and Coventry Technical College (CTC). Students attended three days a week in Birmingham and two days at Coventry. Sean had BSL Stage 2 already so he joined at the point where students progressed from Stages 2 to 3 in April 1988 (the wettest April for one hundred years) but Karen started in September 1988.

From Zero to Hero

The Manpower Service Commission (MSC) promoted the course by saying they could take people with nothing and turn them into fully fledged communicators with BSL Stage 3 'From zero to hero'. However, both Sean and Karen had some sign language skills already. Sean's career route had started at the RNID's 'Court Grange', a residential centre where he worked on producing videos and subtitles. He asked if they would allow him three months to learn sign language. They agreed and sent him on a total immersion course over several weekends where it was strictly 'voice–off'. Sean, like many others, was hooked. Then he went to work for the London Deaf Video Project (LDVP) aiming to become a TV producer. By that time Sean had BSL Stage 2, but he began to realise he wanted more – he wanted to be an interpreter. The problem was, at that time

BSL Stage 3 courses were few and far between, so the CSW course was ideal – a way to get funded to achieve BSL Stage 3. So Sean made his way to Birmingham. Karen didn't have good enough A level results for university, so did voluntary work for a while, and attended BSL evening classes. She had been 'signing-on' to the unemployment register for about a year and a half, when the employment centre told her, 'You need to find a job. You can work in a bar' – it was the impetus she needed to look for something better. She thought initially of a travel and tourism course at a local college, and had a brief dream of supplying tourism for Deaf people. But then the CSW course cropped up.

The Birmingham CSW Course

Birmingham was the only place to offer the intense '9 to 5' training, with funding. Karen commented that it seems strange now to think that the training took place in Birmingham, because London has always been the place where everything happens. However, it was convenient because she lived in Dudley, just down the road. She could still claim her dole money, and because she was on the course she received £10 a week on top of that – but it wasn't enough and she had to dig into her own pockets through the course with the prospect of a job at the end. To be eligible for MSC funding, academic institutions were required to support the training. Deaf people were attending Coventry Technical College (CTC), so some people were working there in a communication role already. The first CSW course had run the previous year (1986-87) at Bournville College, but ceased when one of the main lecturers moved to a new job in Coventry. A joint proposal therefore was made between CTC and the Birmingham Institute for the Deaf (BID) and was successful. It is almost ironic that the first centre to pilot the new CSW qualification in 2010 was City College Coventry, because that is where CSW training had started over twenty years ago. It is also interesting that Christine Reeves, who was a freelance tutor on the original course, remained at Coventry College for many years. Sadly Christine passed away in December 2011. She is remembered fondly by many.

Deaf Tutors. Christine Reeves taught at Coventry, and Karl Channer, Bill Channings, Roger Sutton and Denis Shilston all taught at Bournville and were involved in BID. The Deaf tutors were also used as role models. They were all at the heart of the Deaf Community. Karen commented that the students almost hero-worshipped those 'Deaf luminaries'. At that time, Deaf people were beginning to be trained as teachers. Both Sean and Karen remember that Christine was a stunning, beautiful signer. She was the lead tutor, and it seemed she was the only tutor to have the British Sign Language Training Agency (BSLTA) quali-fication (The British Deaf Association established the BSLTA in 1985 at the University of Durham, for training Deaf people to teach sign language). It was the time that Clark Denmark was developing the BSLTA with the Durham University British Sign Language Teacher Training Centre (DUBSLTTC).

Hearing tutors. Warren Nickerson and Robin Caley taught at Bournville College, and subsequently Coventry College (Sean recalls that Robin Caley was the main impetus for the course. He was the Chair of BID at the time). Mike Preston, also at Bournville and Coventry College, was a social worker with the Deaf.

A Learning Curve for the Tutors

Because it was a new course, it seemed that the tutors were on their own learning curve. They set few written assignments, if any, and the course was structured much like a modern

National Vocational Qualification (NVQ). The course was long and immersive with tutors constantly revisiting and reinforcing sign language skills, and there was a strong recommendation to attend Deaf clubs, and to get involved in anything and everything Deaf. Most of the focus was on practical skills, but there were also week-long skills sessions where specialists were brought in to present different topics. There was a Lipspeaking course and a teaching unit (Part 1 of the City and Guilds 7307 Teacher Training Certificate). As part of that module, Sean did a teaching placement in Braidwood School for the Deaf. Karen went to Nottingham Deaf Society regularly once a week, then five weeks placement at the Royal Association for the Deaf (RAD) in Acton, London, lodging with a friend.

Some of the week-long specialisms:

1. **Lipspeaking.**
2. **Deafblind guiding.**
3. **Notetaking.** This was not like modern notetaking, where notes are given at the end of a session. Students took the notes away and typed them up later.
4. **Teeline.** This was a style of shorthand alphabet, fashionable at the time, but was not popular within the cohort. Eventually only one student went on to use it.
5. **CLAIT.** This was a version of the computing course that is still around today (Computer Literacy and Information Technology). The cohort was brought up to a certain level in order to support Deaf students.

Personal Reminiscences and Views

Sean recalls that it didn't feel like a college course; it seemed like the students were guinea pigs being spruced up for the local pet show. It felt like something special. They had the thrilling impression that the cohort would become part of Deaf history

– it was such a crucial time – 1987 was the year the Association of Sign Language Interpreters (ASLI) was born. It was like Huxley's 'brave new world', but it had a similar undercurrent of dread because Warren Nickerson and Robin Caley received an immense amount of criticism from interpreters. The British Deaf Association (BDA) had its own interpreters, but when the new CSWs finished the training and came out with Stage 3 BSL, they were entitled to be paid £13 an hour (possibly MSC funded) – that was more money than the interpreters, who were more highly skilled. So the question was asked, 'Who are these communicators who think they are something special?' Warren and Robin were accused of the impossible – attempting to create interpreters in a year. Sean's view is that CSWs spend most of their time interpreting, but the newly qualified CSWs were not able to become qualified interpreters for a number of years.

A Stern Warning from Interpreters

Karen remembers interpreters from Sean's course entering her class and delivering a traumatic warning that the course would not make them interpreters. It was daunting yet challenging, and the students felt they had a lot to prove. It was a worrying time, with backstabbing, criticism and pressure. It felt like it was all directed at the students on the CSW course, and some people hoped they would fail spectacularly. The CSW role was constantly drummed into the students. But Karen thought 'I don't want to have a role. I want to impart language and that's it.' Interpreting was seen as the natural progression – it was just progressing from one role to another. Karen remembers thinking, 'I don't quite like this education thing, I'd rather go with people to the doctor's'. Sean remembers realising that it was all about language and that it is important to be skilled in two languages because CSWs were interpreting what the teacher said for the student. Sean comments that the same discussions about defining the CSW role are happening now, with the same points being debated. Karen agrees that nothing has changed, with articles and interpreter forums discussing the same issues as twenty years ago; 'New people come in and join the same old arguments'.

After qualifying, Karen worked just four months as a CSW. She qualified in September 1989, starting work immediately in Bournville College. It was an interesting time for her. They had a lot of Deaf students, but Karen worked with a handful of the more challenging, minimal language students with disabilities. Karen remembers wanting to spend more time in education, possibly staying at Bournville, but four months later was offered a job with the Royal National Institute for Deaf People (RNID) Interpreting Unit in Manchester. She started there in January 1990, and the RNID fast-tracked her on their own courses and she became a qualified interpreter a year and a half later. She remembers having a passion to get where she wanted. She was briefly the youngest qualified interpreter at 23, but Jemina Napier qualified at the age of 21 the following year. Sean lasted slightly longer as a CSW than Karen. He was a freelance CSW straight after the course and for about a year relied on income from just two students, but his reputation as an interpreter grew as he did increasingly more interpreting work. He went on to train at Durham and was a qualified interpreter a year and a half later. It meant that both Karen and Sean qualified as interpreters in 1992.

Where Are You Now?

Sean and Karen are co-owners of Sign Solutions, one of the largest British Sign Language Interpreting agencies in the UK.

Sign Solutions is also a Signature Accredited NVQ training centre, offering BSL training and assessment from Level 1 to Level 6, as well as the NVQ Level 6 BSL/English Interpreting. Even though Sign Solutions can offer opportunities for their candidates to collect evidence for their portfolios, it's nothing like the almost 24/7 access to Deaf people that Sean and Karen had on their training courses. It's tough now and Karen realises just how lucky they were back then on the CSW course.

In the Beginning: I Was There

Tracey Pycroft

Interview: Monday 31st October 2011, via Skype

To set the scene, 1989 was the year that the Berlin wall fell. That momentous event was in the news around the time that Tracey Pycroft's training commenced at Barry College, South Glamorgan, Wales. She was one of the students on the new CSW course, recently inaugurated, although she was largely unaware of the significance of her decision to attend the course (in that hers was one of the first cohorts). It seemed a natural thing to do, gaining the qualification and becoming a CSW in education. The course was intensive and full-time, and ran from September 1989 to June 1990. It was originally funded by the Manpower Services Commission which by that time changed to the 'Training Agency'.

Sign Language Naïve

Tracey had done no sign language before she started the course, but had a determination to work with Deaf people. This was because in her first job after school with an insurance company, she had been given the task of dealing with a customer who was Deaf. She had no training or knowledge, but she wasn't afraid and received such a 'buzz'. At the end the customer said 'Thank you', and Tracey recalls it was the best day of the four and half years that she had worked there – she had fallen in love with BSL. She found a course at Redbridge Technical College in East London but failed to get past the interview. She was told she was too young at 21, and that she didn't have the necessary life experience. Barry College however, held a different view and offered her a place, but there was a problem – the entry requirements for the Barry course were that candidates were unemployed. Tracey decided (together with a number of others at the time) to make herself unemployed in order to be eligible for the course. She didn't care for her job, so making herself unemployed was not traumatic – she was determined to work with Deaf people. It seems that the government's initiative for getting unemployed people off the register was unsophisticated.

Emphasis on BSL

Tracey duly started the course and discovered very soon that there was a big emphasis on learning BSL – 13 hours per week of BSL training. There were also several other modules. The modules were as follows:

1. **Deafness Studies.** Various guest speakers talked about their lives as Deaf people. There was a range of grass roots Deaf people and those who had been to university.
2. **Deaf People in the Community.** Students learned about where Deaf people could be found; Deaf clubs, care homes, hospitals (hearing tests). It was an eclectic mix of culture and audiology, but the emphasis was on audiology. To Tracey, at the time, it didn't seem unusual.
3. **Language and Communication.** This focused on issues surrounding BSL.
4. **Lipspeaking.** This was a one week block with an exam at the end.
5. **Deafblind manual.** Students were trained to Level 1.
6. **Paget Gorman (PG).** Students were trained in PG and other English-based sign systems.

7. **Human Growth and Development.** This was audiology again: how the ear grows and develops, and childhood illnesses affecting hearing. Students learned about hearing loss not being loss of speech only, but also environmental. That had a big effect on Tracey, and was an experience she will always remember.

8. **Support Strategies and Notetaking.** The Role of the Communicator.

9. **British Sign Language.**

The Stage 1 BSL training commenced in September. Students were required to attend Deaf clubs one night a week in preparation for the exam in December. The exams filled the students with dread, and there was only one opportunity to do it right first time, but thankfully, Tracey passed. The Stage 2 exam took place in March 1990. Tracey was again successful, together with one other student who had Deaf parents. After passing Stage 2 they were required to attend Deaf Clubs two nights a week, or on Saturday. The tutors then concentrated on the other students, getting them up to Stage 2, with the two Stage 2 holders helping with video work. The course was somewhat lacking in formal teaching at Stage 3. The training was mostly through videos, usually of Clark Denmark, and students were told it was mandatory to mix with the Deaf community two evenings a week and work in the local school for Deaf Children as part of their placements. Tracey passed two of the four parts of the Stage 3 exam, but by then the CSW course had finished, so she went to evening classes, successfully re-sitting the outstanding two parts in October. It meant that Tracey had gone from sign language-naïve to Stage 3 within eighteen months.

Tracey recalls that what she learnt on the course is still relevant to her job now, and that it is a bonus to have so much background knowledge, which was imparted by a group of very high quality tutors and lecturers.

Deaf Tutors

- **Sheila Moon.** She taught sign language throughout the year. She brought in many of her Deaf friends, and also used videos.
- **Tony Troy.** He was from South Wales, a social worker with Deaf people and a Deaf interpreter. At that time, social workers for Deaf people, as part of the job, were given the opportunity to become interpreters (it seemed without training). Some students did work experience with him.
- **Selina.** She had Usher Syndrome. Tracey can't recall her surname. She helped in some sessions and the students worked with her in the community sometimes.

Lecturers

- **Sian Tesni.** Sian was responsible for setting up the course, and she was the coordinator. She was passionate about whatever she was teaching, and her enthusiasm was infectious. Students seemed to pay more attention because her way of teaching was not to simply reel off material from a blackboard or overheads – she genuinely believed in it.
- **Karen Every-Clayton.** Karen later joined the committee of NATED.

Work Experience Placements

Tracey remembers the work experiences vividly because they were varied and challenging.

1. **Holiday Home.** A week placement in a holiday home for elderly people was arranged, linked to the Deafblind module. It was thought that some people there were Deafblind, but in reality, some elderly ladies were losing

their sight and hearing through age, and did not have congenital Deafblindness.

2. **Hospital audiology department.** This was a one day visit. The whole group spent a day in the audiology department, and underwent the hearing tests. One student was informed that he had quite a severe hearing loss. He was unaware of it and was traumatised. He felt that he could not continue and eventually left the course. Tracey mused that perhaps he thought that if his hearing was not up to standard, he could not support Deaf students.

3. **Hospital audiology clinic.** This was a six-week block working in a local hospital audiology clinic for one day a week. This involved the making of moulds and the fitting and adjustment of hearing aids etc. It was a good opportunity to converse with people about how they felt going through the process and how they felt about their hearing loss.

4. **Local school for Deaf children.** This was a six-week block for a day a week in a local school with Deaf children. It was useful for practising BSL, but for Tracey it was difficult because the ethos was 'Total Communication'. The teacher instructed Tracey to sign and speak at the same time, but that was in direct conflict to learning BSL because that required voices to be 'off'.

5. **Shadowing.** The shadowing was of a social worker for Deaf people. This involved home visits to Deaf people. Students aided the filling in of forms and paperwork, and arranged for flashing lights and minicoms etc.

6. **Outdoor Pursuits Course.** This was a one week course with children from the county. The role was a volunteer communicator as part of work experience. It was a revelation because of the children's different communication needs, and some had additional disabilities. Tracey had been

trained in BSL by adults, so this was a new experience and helped her to differentiate between Deaf people and their communication methods.

Tracey passed the course, but there was a hitch at the end because the college had failed to validate the course. The students were expecting a BTEC award, but the processes had not been completed in time, so they were presented with a college certificate. In July 1997, seven years later, the awarding body ran a mop-up exercise for people without the proper accreditation. Students were asked to submit files of work from 1989/90, and informed of any additional work to meet the new requirements (one or two essays). Tracey did the extra work and now proudly holds a BTEC Certificate that bears the words 'Caring (Communication Support Worker)'. The certificate was issued by Bournville College of Further Education.

After Qualifying

After leaving Barry College, Tracey applied to a local service near her home in Bridgend to support Deaf students in colleges, county-wide. She was offered the job and was there from September to March, working part-time, commuting between three different colleges during the week supporting various students. This was a valuable experience, meeting different Deaf students and staff, and forming life-long friendships. She then took time-out for travelling, and while in Australia, received a call from Sian Tesni, co-ordinator of the CSW course. There was a job at Barry College, full-time, but the applicants hadn't been suitable. Tracey was offered and accepted the job which lasted full-time until taking maternity leave in 1994. After her daughter was born, Tracey went back with slightly reduced hours and stayed on a part-time basis until 1997. Before she left the CSW job, Tracey successfully finished the

RNID 'Introduction to Interpreting' course in 1994, becoming a registered trainee.

Other Students in the Cohort

The cohort consisted of ten students. One left because of a hearing loss. One other, who had Deaf parents, did well on the course, but she didn't go on to become an interpreter. Two others did some CSW work. One of those started working as a CSW in Mid Glamorgan then moved away. Another student named Lynne worked as a CSW at Barry College with Tracey. Later she did a Special Educational Needs degree and became a Teacher of the Deaf, then became Head of Service in a High School unit for Deaf children. Tracey continued working with Deaf people, as did Paul Beckett (now retired) who came from a social work background. After completing the course he went back to being a social worker with Deaf people. Of the cohort of ten, as far as she knows, Tracey was the only one who continued as a CSW and then went on to become an interpreter.

For Tracey, the audiology module, despite other people thinking it was boring, was an important focus for her, including Deaf Awareness delivered by Deaf people. There was information about the medical model of Deafness and then about Deafness in the community. It was very beneficial knowing how the ear works, including the names of the bones in the ear, and that knowledge has stayed with Tracey.

Tracey believes that she started interpreting as a CSW too soon. They were constantly told that they were not interpreters, but Tracey had interpreting as an aim. She believes that what CSWs do in a classroom is interpreting, so she wishes that there had been more about interpreting on the course. For years, working as a CSW, she wasn't sure that what she was doing was correct. It was later in interpreter training she realised that much of what she did was actually OK. Tracey wonders how long it would take to gain an equal amount of knowledge from a contemporary course, bearing in mind the course was full time, 5 days a week with extra-curricular activities also.

Training Journey After the Course

Tracey qualified as an interpreter in 2000 through the graduate interpreter programme by the CACDP. At that time NVQs hadn't been introduced, so many budding interpreters were rushing around doing every short course available, linked to interpreting, but couldn't achieve qualification. Tracey did an interpreter course through the RNID in 1993/94, then the Bristol University Horizon course. This had European funding, and was for people who were already working as interpreters. It started as a week block in December 1997, in the interpreting studies department at Bristol University. Students were sent home with various assignments to write, which were marked and returned. Then there was a final week block at the end of the academic year. Students received a certificate in advanced interpreting.

BSL Futures Project, Wales

Tracey is also an A1 Assessor and a trained mentor for ASLI. In 2005/6 she underwent the Post Graduate Diploma in interpreting, to top up her interpreting theory, and became the senior interpreter on the BSL Futures Project in Wales (2006-8) where she was responsible for five supervisors and twelve apprentices. This project was modelled on the early CSW course. Tracey worked on the project as a senior interpreter partly because she had the knowledge from the CSW course.

I Was There 89

The project entry requirement was Level 2 BSL, and for two years, students were given the same intense experience as the CSW course. Some material was replicated and some was changed, but it was more interpreter-focused, rather than CSW focused. Thirty people started the course, but two dropped out, with everyone else going on to become qualified interpreters. The worry was that existing interpreters would experience a decline in work because of the new interpreters being trained, and initially there was a drop in demand. It was hoped that they would be trained to work in public services, such as hospitals and police, although not in custodial situations. Initially the newer interpreters struggled to find work, but it evened out and everyone has enough work within South Wales.

Where Are You Now?

Tracey works as a self-employed interpreter, but is involved with other projects, including mentoring speech-to-text reporters for Signature, and guiding them through the assessment process. Also for Signature she is involved in writing the National Occupational Standards for Lipspeakers (she holds the Level 3 lipspeaking qualification herself). She is also tutoring people doing NVQ Levels 3 and 6 qualifications with Sign Solutions. However, despite all this varied activity, education remains as one of Tracey's favourite domains, and one that she feels most comfortable in, especially university level.

4
Politics
The political background to the initial CSW courses

The trajectory of the Manpower Services Commission (MSC) was short and bright. It was set up by the Conservative Party, with Edward Heath as Prime Minister, under the Employment and Training Act 1973, to develop a comprehensive manpower strategy for Britain and to advise the Secretary of State on employment matters.

The MSC consisted of nine members and a chairperson, all appointed by the Secretary of State:
- Three members represented the interests of employees,
- Three represented the interests of employers,
- Two consulted with local authority associations, and
- One represented professional education interests.

In addition to training, the MSC's functions included responsibility through the Training Services Agency for jobcentres. The first official jobcentre appeared in April 1973 in Reading,

Berkshire, the same year that Britain joined the European Economic Community (EEC). The Conservative party lost the general election in 1974 and the Labour party, with Harold Wilson as Prime Minister, took control. By 1975 four hundred jobcentres had been opened.

Change of Political Landscape

When Harold Wilson resigned as Prime Minister in 1976, he was replaced by James Callaghan who remained in power until 1979 when the Conservative party, with Margaret Thatcher as their leader, won the next general election. Margaret Thatcher remained as Prime Minister until 1990.

As with most of the developed world, recession hit the United Kingdom at the turn of the 1980s. When Margaret Thatcher became Prime Minister the country had just witnessed the Winter of Discontent in which numerous public sector workers had staged strikes and inflation was high. Mrs Thatcher's battle against inflation resulted in the closure of many inefficient factories, shipyards and coal mines - mostly during her first four-year term in power. These drastic measures did reduce inflation, but resulted in unemployment being at an all time high of 3,000,000 by January 1982 - a level not seen for some 50 years (Wikipedia [online, n.d.]).

By 1982 the Thatcher government was highly unpopular. Soaring inflation and a massive increase in unemployment made it seem unlikely that she would win a second term. However, because (it is claimed) Mrs Thatcher was able to play the part of the heroic war leader in the Falklands War between March and June 1982, the Conservative party achieved a landslide in the 1983 general election (Gillard, 2001).

When responsibility for the Employment Service Division was transferred to the MSC, administrative responsibility for all its local offices was centralised under a Chief Executive. David (later Lord) Young became the Chief Executive in 1983.

Demise of the Jobcentre Network

The national jobcentre network and the functions of the Employment and Enterprise Group of the Commission were taken from the control of the MSC in October 1987. This coincided with the start of the second year of the CSW training project. The first cohort were trained during the academic year 1986-87.

Having lost its employment functions, the focus of the MSC was concentrated on the government's training and vocational education programme, and it was re-named Training Commission in May 1988. But barely five months later, in September 1988, the Training Commission was abolished, and the Training Agency was created to perform its functions within the Employment Department Group. The Training Agency was in turn wound up in November 1990 and re-integrated into the Employment Department.

The MSC was a like a sun-flare that glowed quick and bright, then faded – the MSC, together with its available funds for the training of CSWs, amongst many other worthy projects, had disappeared by 1988. Some of the reports in this book speak of the MSC existing after 1988. This must be due both to the fact that the machinations of government do not immediately filter down to the population, and to the passage of years affecting memory.

David Young, the High Flyer

For the purpose of this study, the years during which David Young was the Chief Executive are the most interesting. One political commentator has said of Young's time in charge that they were: 'Breathtaking years of stewardship and expansion from 1983 to 1987' (Ashford, 1989). Margaret Thatcher famously remarked of him: 'Others bring me problems. David brings me solutions'. When he moved on from the MSC in September 1984, David Young entered the Lords and joined the Cabinet as Minister without Portfolio, becoming Secretary of State for Employment in 1985. 1990 saw the publication of his book 'The Enterprise Years'. In June 2010 he was appointed 'Enterprise Czar' by Prime Minister David Cameron.

'Staggering' Amounts of Money

But in what respect were those years so spectacular, and did the initial CSW course owe all its resources ultimately to David Young? A look at the budgets will enlighten:

The MSC's first full year's spend (1972-73) was a meagre £125 million (Scott, 1986).

The budget for the year 1984-85 (the budget that was set in the year Young took the helm) was a staggering £2072 million (Scott, 1986). This budget was used for disparate projects such as cafes, museums, social enterprises, books and training. Funding for training which concentrated on improving employment prospects, especially for disabled people, (including Deaf people) were known as Innovation Projects.

Green and Nickerson report on the background to the funding for support for Deaf people at this time, from their perspective:

'During the period 1983-85 the major national organisations in response to requests from Deaf people, were pressing for support for Deaf people. More specifically, that monies be made available for such. Much of this pressure focused upon the MSC during their review of the provision for Deaf people in 1984.' (Green and Nickerson,

1992, p47).

Green and Nickerson also state that they did not know the details of the submissions made to the MSC by organisations such as the British Deaf Association (BDA) and the Royal National Institute for Deaf People (RNID). Perhaps Stewart Simpson, as Chief Executive of the Council for the Advancement of Communication with Deaf People (CACDP) at that time had a better insight into the situation as he describes the process in more detail (Simpson, 2007).

Green and Nickerson report that, in 1985, the MSC announced plans for a two year Youth Training Scheme in a Government White Paper (April 1985) entitled 'Education Training of Young People'. After much pressure from leading national organisations representing Deaf people, the MSC had agreed to make special provision and funding for Deaf students (Green and Nickerson, 1992). This news was very welcome but, it also raised concerns about who would be able to offer communication support to the anticipated number of Deaf young people who would want to take part in this training. It was already common knowledge at time that Teachers of the Deaf (ToDs) were struggling to cope with the increase in the number of Deaf school leavers wanting to continue into further education. Something radical needed to happen.

In July 1985, following proposals for the establishment of a Communication and Support Service which would provide a range of services for Deaf youngsters on Youth Training Schemes (YTS), a meeting was held which highlighted concerns about the lack of qualified interpreters. The number of young Deaf people wanting to enter training schemes or further education was by far exceeding the number of qualified interpreters available to offer communication support to them. MSC were informed of the concerns, especially of the length of time it takes to train interpreters and, following a great deal of correspondence, MSC asked if there was any way in which they could help to alleviate the shortage of interpreters.

At this point, following discussions with Robin Caley, as Chairman of the Council for Advancement of Communication with Deaf People (CACDP), but also as Director of Birmingham Institute for the Deaf (BID), and Warren Nickerson, a lecturer with responsibility for Deaf students at Bournville College of Further Education, Birmingham, CACDP submitted four possible schemes of training communicators/interpreters to the MSC (Simpson, 2007).

Funding For Training Initiatives

The training was to be funded as an Innovation Project.

Funding was granted to support two of the proposals:
1. 26 week pilot scheme
2. 13 week 'follow-on' pilot scheme for those who reached a specified standard.

Training was to be full-time, Monday to Friday with three days per week being spent at Bournville College and two days per week attending BID to improve sign language and mix with members of the Deaf Community.

In order to qualify for the MSC funding, applicants needed to match the following criteria:
- Be registered as unemployed before training began
- Be aged between 19 and 30
- Preferably have a minimum five G.C.E. 'O' Levels including English Language

The intake was limited to twelve students, but applications far exceeded this number.

Other schemes which attracted funding under the umbrella of Innovation Project included:
- The training of Deaf people in Leeds to deliver Deaf

Awareness training (Miranda Pickersgill, interview 2011).

- The first pictorial sign language dictionary 'Communication Link' published in 1985 by Cath Smith and Terry Morris, Head Teacher of Beverley School for the Deaf, Middlesbrough (Cath Smith, interview 2011).

One can only guess at the immense cost of running such a full time course. To be awarded such funding appears to have been a complete and utter luxury. Perhaps, at the time, the funding was accepted as the norm. It does seem somewhat incongruous that, at a time of high unemployment and inflation, so much money was available for training. It would appear that the vision was that such training would equip more people for employment, hence reducing the number of unemployed.

In the present financial climate (2012) under the leadership of the current Conservative/Liberal Democrat coalition (or as some wags have called it - the Con/Dem government), with cuts being made to funding from every angle, the relatively high costs of offering training is proving to be prohibitive. This has limited the number of centres in a position to offer CSW training, and the number of candidates able to access it. The problem is not candidate apathy, but with current high levels of unemployment and increased insecurity around employment, self funding or funding by employers is becoming increasingly difficult. One can only hope that the funding situation will improve so that more people can take advantage of the training now on offer.

5
CSW Training Continues

Training for communication support workers has been in existence, in one guise or another since the development of the initial training courses in the late 1980s. In 1992 the training was accredited by BTEC (Business and Technicians Education Council) which changed its name to Edexcel in 1996. This accreditation gave the qualification national recognition for the first time and enabled students and colleges to claim funding for the training, which was vital if the qualification was to remain viable.

The CSW qualification underwent a number of changes over the years, both in terms of structure and title. Some of the amendments were needed in response to changing in funding regulations by the Further Education Funding Council (FEFC) from time to time. As most of the centres delivering the Edexcel CSW qualification were FE colleges, the funding status of a qualification was vitally important. Examples regarding the change in title of the qualification are shown below:

Between 1992 and June 1997 the title was:
BTEC Continuing Education Certificate in Caring - Communication Support Work with Deaf People.

From September 1997 the title changed to:
Edexcel Professional Development Award - Communication Support Workers with Deaf People.

From September 1998 the title changed again to:
Edexcel Professional Development Award - Communication Support Workers with Deaf Students.

Edexcel continued to accredit the qualification until, due to the ever decreasing number of candidates, it was finally removed from Edexcel's qualification portfolio in 2010.

At this point, even though attempts had been made for the new CSW qualification to be accredited jointly by Edexcel and Signature, from September 2010 Signature became the sole awarding organisation to provide a nationally recognised qualification for CSWs by including the following award in their qualification portfolio:

Level 3 Certificate in Learning Support (Communication Support Workers).

The latest news regarding changes to the CSW qualification, at time of writing is as follows: The government's Standards and Qualifications function transferred from LLUK (Lifelong Learning UK) to LSIS (Learning and Skills Improvement Service) on 1 April 2011. Many of the units in the Signature

CSW qualification were then revised but awarding organisations, including Signature, were not consulted at this time. The core units of the CSW qualification are in the process of being revised again and Signature and other awarding organisations have been asked to respond to the proposals and to new guidance materials. It is unlikely this will have any major implications for CSW candidates but would make the structure of the units more compliant with Ofqual's requirements for unit writing.

In addition, following guidance from LSIS, the title of the Signature CSW qualification will change to Level 3 Certificate in Communication Support for D/deaf Learners with effect from September 2012.

It must be acknowledged that, for a variety of reasons, some institutions and training organisations have offered their own training of CSWs over the years. The training was often accredited, but not nationally recognised. Examples include Exeter Royal Academy of Deaf Education (ERADE) who adapted an OCN (Open College Network) qualification and trained their CSWs in-house. The Sensory Support Service in Surrey have also trained their support staff using another OCN qualification, specifically adapted to suit their needs. Their support staff are given the title of Student Support Workers (SSWs) and are trained to provide communication support to both Deaf and/ or visually impaired students. This qualification was developed because it was considered there was nothing available to meet the needs of the employer in this area. Even though it is accepted that the training is not nationally recognised, support staff are trained to the precise needs of their employer.

Without a doubt there will be many other examples of such training taking place throughout the UK. Failing to mention a particular centre where CSW training occurred should in no way be taken as an indication of their standard of training.

Miranda Pickersgill, former Chief Executive, CACDP

Miranda recalls that she was always consulting with Edexcel. Soon after being appointed at CACDP, Edexcel contacted her and pointed out that they had so few centres that they couldn't really afford to keep running the CSW course. She sympathised because she knew how much it costs to keep the infrastructure for a qualification where you've only got a few candidates every year. Certain centres were saying 'Could you just get this lot through?' Edexcel did let people go through the old qualification. Miranda recalls one year where there were only a few centres left offering the Edexcel qualification. CACDP then started to talk more specifically, not about the registration, but about qualifications. One proposal at that time was that the CSW qualification should be jointly awarded with language and communication qualifications to be awarded by CACDP and a educational and professional qualification that was going to be awarded by Edexcel.

Edexcel had some existing post-16 non-teaching qualifications. Later CACDP looked at what they also had at pre-16 to see if this would work in a joint award. From what was on the shelves already, Edexcel already had units on professional practice in education. CACDP saw as their responsibility a unit of a qualification that was about professional practice, as it related to working with Deaf people. For example, CACDP had some consultancy money to pay people like Rachel O'Neill to write a professional practice unit. These people were working for CACDP and by the time Miranda left CACDP at the end of 2006, there were written units for virtually everything concerning CSW qualifications that was CACDP's responsibility. It was then expected that they would be submitted for accreditation. Edexcel, within their qualification, would have units that were about professional practice and working in education. The potential was there to have - not a joint award - joint awards suddenly became unfashionable - but an award from two different awarding bodies. The views of the Qualifications and Curriculum Authority (QCA) had to be taken into account also. A discussion was starting to take place around how candidates could meet the requirements and become eligible should registration ever take place. That was the framework.

Rob Rodgers is another professional who was involved in the training of CSWs for a number of years, both as a lecturer and as an external verifier for Edexcel. Rob shares his experiences here:

Rob Rodgers

Rob Rodgers - Former external verifier (EV) for Edexcel. Interview: Thursday 8 March 2012, Derby College

Far from it being a lifelong dream, Rob Rodgers had no intention of specialising as a Teacher of the Deaf (ToD) when he first qualified as a teacher in 1982 through an In-service training course at the school he was working in. Interestingly there was hardly any mention of British Sign Language on the course. Rob claims that he almost 'fell into' the role of a ToD when some friends at the church he attended had seen a vacancy advertised and commented that they felt that this was something that might suit him.

Rob's first teaching post was at the Royal School for the Deaf in Derby, working within the secondary department. He remained at the school for approximately four years, working in both the primary and secondary departments. Whilst there he also provided some tutorials within the Further Education (FE) department. He well remembers being told at his interview that as long as he spoke clearly, the profoundly Deaf children would understand him.

Following this, in 1984 Rob went to work for the Nottingham Hearing Impaired Service which was still very local geographically to where Rob lived in the Derby area. Whilst working in the FE sector in Nottingham, Rob came into contact with various people, including Chris Green and learnt about some of the work Chris was involved in with the Working Hands Project. Rob recalls that attending a Manpower Services Commission (MSC) course on 'support workers' made him start thinking about the whole area of communication support workers (CSWs).

A little while later, Rob started working for Derbyshire Services for the Hearing Impaired in the FE section. This role included working in colleges in Derby and setting up support services for Deaf students within the locality and building on the work that Chris Green had started for the service. Around this time, Rob became involved with CACDP (Council for the Advancement of Communication with Deaf People) and the CSW qualification. The qualification was offered at Derby College, with an intake each year for approximately two or three years. In 1997 Rob was offered a post working for Derby College for Deaf people as their Training and Development Manager. One of the things that the Principal, Brenda Mullen, was keen for Rob to be involved in was the training of CSWs. Rob's post was income generating, which means that he was expected to make contact with external organisations and take on additional work which would, in turn, generate an additional income for the school. This enabled Rob to take on the role of external verifier for BTEC (Business and Technicians Education Council which later became Edexcel).

As external verifier, Rob had responsibility for working with between twelve and fourteen centres who were teaching the CSW qualification. The work was shared with Carrie MacHattie who later had to step down as external verifier as a result of other commitments. Rob's role involved visiting centres, verifying candidates' work and ultimately recommending (or not) candidates for certification as CSWs. During this time, Rob made contact with another external verifier called Julie Coombes. Rob recalls that Julie was working for Mary Hare Grammar School and was keen to develop training for CSWs who worked in an oral background. Rob and Julie discovered that, around this time, CACDP were beginning to work with Deaf Educational Instructors and were discussing the development of bilingual CSWs. Rob recalls that a lot of initiatives were starting to develop at the time. It all felt very exciting. CACDP were very keen on developing units under the leadership of Miranda Pickersgill. Rob recalls that Mickey Vale who had worked with Miranda in Leeds, had been given funding by CACDP to develop some units for CSWs. Due to the changes within the Further Education Funding Council (FEFC) regulations, it became clear that the existing CSW qualification would soon cease to attract funding so changes needed to be made. Rob's involvement with Edexcel therefore changed and he was asked to focus on a new format for CSW training in order to meet the new funding requirements.

Edexcel and CACDP Working Closely Together

At this time CACDP and Edexcel were working closely together to develop new units for the CSW qualification. Edexcel were keen to continue to award the qualification, but were aware that it would need to be updated to meet the new demands of the new FEFC regulations. Rob was very keen to include the major work that was being carried out by two of CACDP's working parties at that time.

A representative from Edexcel, Barbara Molog, started working with Rob and the working parties concerned. Barbara was instrumental in merging the new ideas that were evolving from the working parties with the new regulations from FEFC. From 2000 Rob, Julie Coombes and Barbara Molog worked together to develop new units to meet the new requirements. In Rob's opinion, problems started to arise when the format of the CSW qualification started to change and a number of new units were introduced. The new training included units for monolingual CSWs, bilingual CSWs and Deaf Educational Instructors. Unfortunately, even though all these new units were being developed, Edexcel decided that there was not enough of a business case for them to continue to offer the qualification within their portfolio. Rob recalls this as quite a sad time in Deaf education when things became quite acrimonious and there was a lot of ill feeling generated by, in Rob's opinion, conflicting aspirations concerning where the CSW training could go, where it should go and where the Government funding was needing it to be taken. Funding was an important factor from Edexcel's perspective. As a business which focuses on training, a business case could only be considered if a qualification qualified for FEFC funding, particularly at Award level, Certificate level and Diploma level, within their framework.

Over a period of approximately two years, various people were working on trying to develop units and a qualification for CSWs that would fit into Edexcel's framework. CACDP had a CSW working party who worked closely with Rob, Julie Coombes and Barbara Molag, trying to develop an appropriate qualification. Sadly, people had differing aspirations and ideas of how the qualification should develop. There was no allocated leader to guide the parties in any one particular direction. At the time, CACDP were considered to be in a very strong position in order to take the lead on this development. It is possible that the venture could have had a very different outcome, had CACDP taken on the leadership role. Unfortunately, what then happened, rather than everyone working together in harmony, was that people took sides and held onto differing views, which led to a very uncomfortable situation.

Understandably, CACDP's main income derived from the British Sign Language (BSL) examinations at Level 1, Level 2 and Level 3. National Vocational Qualifications (NVQs) were also being introduced at this time and, naturally enough, CACDP chose to focus on these areas rather than developing the CSW qualification. From a purely business perspective, there was understandably little incentive for either CACDP or Edexcel to spend too much time or energy on redeveloping the CSW qualification. CSW training was, and always had been, a low income generator, whatever its importance morally. Even at its peak, there were only between fourteen and sixteen centres offering CSW training in any one year. Realistically, this could not possibly compare with the number of candidates under-taking BSL Level 1 or Level 2 training. Despite this level of understanding, it was still very sad to accept that CSW training was considered to be such a low priority by both CACDP and Edexcel.

Register of Interpreters in its Infancy

Around this time, the registration of interpreters was in its infancy and took up a great deal of CACDP's energy and resources. Rob acknowledges that both CACDP and NATED (National Association for Tertiary Education for Deaf People) were taking steps to introduce registration for CSWs, but there were a lot of decisions to be made concerning who exactly should appear on a register. For example, should a CSW with BSL 2 appear on the register if they could work quite effectively in an oral setting? The drive for registration seemed to get lost in the melee of all that was going on at the time. Changes in FEFC regulations and what they were requiring was only adding to the confusion. CACDP were in danger of losing all of their BSL qualifications from the framework so, understandably, all their time and effort had to be focused on making changes to ensure that this did not happen. Similarly, at the same time, Edexcel were having to make changes to all of their qualifications to ensure that they remained on the qualification framework and continue to attract FEFC funding.

Perhaps what was needed was a lobby to raise attention to the training needs of CSWs in education. It would have been useful if, for example, FE institutions had formed a lobby to demand minimum standards for CSWs. It feels as though it was a case of being in the wrong place at the wrong time, as far as CSW training was concerned. 'Inclusion' was big news at the time, so the issue of training for CSWs unfortunately seemed to be pushed to one side as there were, in many people's opinions, more important developments needed. When Edexcel became drawn into political arguments which were being raised by a number of individuals concerning the changes needed in CSW training, understandably Edexcel decided that they did not have the time, or resources, to continue in the face of such resistance. Sadly, things got very messy, very quickly.

Unexpected Changes

In 2003 Derby College for Deaf People (DCDP), where Rob was employed, failed its FEFC inspection and the following year it closed completely, resulting in redundancy for Rob. At this point, Rob's links with Deaf education came to a rather abrupt end. As he had been made redundant, Edexcel did ask Rob to become lead verifier for the CSW qualification. Part of the role would have been to try to bring everything together. At that time Rob was searching for another post, so was not able to continue his links with Edexcel. Sadly, no one seemed willing to work for Edexcel and progress the CSW qualification.

When considering why the number of candidates for CSW training was never very high, Rob suggested that, perhaps, society has lost interest in BSL. Undoubtedly, many people can now use BSL but the numbers of people regularly studying for BSL appears to have reduced. Whilst lack of funding will have affected this, perhaps BSL is no longer seen as the 'trendy' thing to do. Following the 'Princess Diana phase' where, because she was seen using BSL, everyone decided that this was something they wanted to learn, interest appears to have peaked and is now, perhaps, fading.

Following Rob's redundancy in 2004, he was unsure who was working as the external verifier for Edexcel after this date. He recalls that Julie Coombes retired from Mary Hare Grammar School around the same time that he became redundant, and he had heard that she continued with the role. Edexcel continued to offer the qualification for a few years after Rob's involvement. The qualification continued to be offered until 2009, with only two centres offering the course in the academic year 2009-2010. Derby College continued to train CSWs using the Edexcel qualification until 2010.

Whilst working at DCDP, Rob was involved in delivering a range of training courses, thanks to funding from the European Economic Community (EEC) Social Fund. The funding allowed the Communications Agency to be established, which Tracey Kelsall worked for. Funding was granted for the training of lipspeaking, notetaking and CSWs. The aim was to establish a local bank of trained professionals to work with Deaf people. Sadly, when the college closed, the Communications Agency closed too.

Rob mused that, sadly, there never appeared to be a 'champion' for CSWs – someone who would fight for training and improvements. In his opinion, there needed to be someone to do this within the education sector, preferably a mainstream champion – a specialist with the drive to take this forward. Within Edexcel there was no one who had the vision, or the passion, to drive the CSW qualification forward. If progress is to be made, someone has to continue fighting for it to happen and try to make those with authority take notice.

Experiences as an EV?

Rob reflected that there were so many different experiences, both good and bad, whilst working as an external verifier that it is difficult to explain. There were a vast variety of ways that the course was being delivered. It was very much personality led. The courses that appeared to be the strongest were where there was a person with real passion and interest in the course. It seemed to be delivered in quite a few places by ToDs, and ToDs who were reaching a certain age. You got the feeling that the centre/school/college wouldn't feel the same in the next few years. People were coming to the end of their professional careers. Very few Deaf people appeared to be running the courses. Deaf people who did run the training were doing so in isolation. In fact, isolation was one of the main concerns. Centres were not talking to each other, even links with NATED were not established. At the time, NATED did not appear to have a very strong influence on any of the centres. Some centres including Manchester and Derby were very involved with NATED, but many places had no contact at all with NATED.

The quality of the courses and the students varied greatly. Without quoting details, quite a few courses really should not have been allowed to run because they did not meet the quality standards that Edexcel had set at the time. As an external veri-fier, Rob had to recommend that either candidates proceeded to certification or were deferred. In some instances, Rob carried out further visits to ensure that changes had been made, as recommended in the previous visit.

At the time, it could not be assumed that work was going to be of a certain standard. There was no standardisation. Some of the work that was being produced needed a lot of additional input to bring it up to the required standard. Edexcel did not offer training days for centres. In the very early days of CSW training, Chris Green and Warren Nickerson organised training events for centres who were interested in offering the courses. This was funded by CACDP, as far as Rob can recall.

What eventually happened was that teaching materials were getting very out of date. Some centres were still using the same materials that Chris and Warren had written many years before. In some instances, the people delivering the training had not realised that events had progressed and that material needed to be updated. This raised concerns around the quality of the teaching.

In direct comparison, people like Rachel O'Neill were deliv-ering a very high standard of training, constantly updating material and introducing new ideas. Other centres caused grave concerns about the outcomes and the standard of CSWs at the end of the training. This proved to be very difficult for Edexcel who, as the examination board, were put under a great deal of pressure from colleges to ensure that candidates achieved the certificate rather than be deferred, even if the quality was not good enough. Colleges are driven by funding. Students need to be retained and to achieve certification to enable colleges to claim funding.

Rob considers that he met some interesting people whilst working as an external verifier. He also admits that he met many people who seemed to be merely treading water, waiting for retirement.

In summary, Rob felt at one time that an external verifier from Derby College and an external verifier from Mary Hare School with an oral emphasis had the potential to achieve something worthwhile. But sadly, the ideal somehow seemed to lose its way. Sometimes, working in the Deaf world, it seems as though the self destruct button is pressed, followed closely by cries of 'Help!' The message needs to be 'Let's see the big picture here, you've got an opportunity.' At times Rob recalls being made to feel like the 'devil incarnate' for allowing developments to take a certain route. Such was the experience of working as an external verifier for Edexcel.

Where Are You Now?

Rob is currently working as the Director of Learning for SEN and Inclusion at Saint Benedict Catholic School and Performing Arts College in Derby. He still lives in the Derby area with his wife and two sons. Sadly he only has contact with the Deaf community through friends who are Deaf and it is with a mixture of feelings that he looks back on the golden age of communication support workers.

Summary

Training for CSWs has now been offered for over twenty five years. Throughout this time the training has varied in content, structure and name but one thing has remained constant - the end goal: to improve communication for Deaf students and to open up the world of education to them, regardless of their level of hearing loss or ability. It is important never to lose sight of that goal, whatever obstacles are thrown in the way.

Presently, in 2012, there is a nationally recognised qualification for CSWs, there are National Occupational Standards (NOS) and there is the possibility of a registration category within the National Registers for Communication Professionals With Deaf People (NRCPD). In theory it seems as though the situation has indeed improved. Only time will tell if this is true. Perhaps in twenty five years' time another book will be published to chart the progress made and celebrate the golden jubilee of the CSWs.

6
I Was There: Professionals

Miranda Pickersgill

Interview: Thursday 3 November 2011, Oxford

Miranda Pickersgill is a very well known and highly respected figure who has featured prominently in the education of Deaf children and adults since the early 1970s.

In 1973 Miranda qualified as a Teacher of the Deaf (ToD). To set the scene, this was the year that Princess Anne married Captain Mark Philips. It was also the year of the three day working week in the UK as a result of high oil and coal prices. Miranda worked in a number of areas including the West Country, Middlesbrough (where she met and formed a long friendship with Cath Smith who was working at Beverley School for the Deaf at the time) and Nottingham.

In 1986, Miranda moved to Leeds as the Teacher of the Deaf with responsibility for establishing post 16 provision for Deaf people, and subsequently for reorganising the service and schools responsible for Deaf children. She was brought in along with some other Deaf and hearing colleagues, including Judith Collins who moved to the University of Durham in 1991, to make that provision. Around this time there were changes within the mainstream education settings (in further education and schools) that were, in a sense, nothing to do with Deaf education, but suddenly there was an awareness of the need for changes within Deaf education also.

Warren & Chris: Visionaries

Quite soon it seemed that young Deaf people aged 16 and above had expectations that they wanted to go into further education (FE), and the staff supporting them also aspired to work in FE. In Miranda's view, what then happened thanks to visionaries like Warren Nickerson and Chris Green, was that to meet this demand, the need for training was identified. However you couldn't start off by saying 'this is what the training is going to be' because there was the issue of 'what exactly is the role going to be?'. It could be said that the role of the communication support worker (CSW) emerged from a negative situation, in that CSWs filled a gap that wasn't being met. Miranda does not feel that was wrong, but CSWs were needed because there wasn't anything else, or because other professionals couldn't deliver what was needed. That in itself created some of the problems.

Miranda acknowledges that it wasn't easy to define the CSW role and develop appropriate training. Models of good practice were emerging, following the Manpower Services Commission (MSC) funded CSW pilot courses which started in Birmingham in 1986. Colleges in Coventry, Derby, Birmingham and Manchester all started to train CSWs. Miranda thinks she remembers them because of people like Chris Green, Warren Nickerson, Rachel O'Neill and Tracey Kelsall. Consequently, in Miranda's opinion, these outstanding people, who emerged at that time and understood what was needed, got on with it and pulled together with the availability of MSC funding.

In Miranda's view, those people were vitally important at that time because of all the things that happened subsequently; all the jealousies and the petty falling out within the field of Deaf education. The post 16, FE Deaf people appeared to be working closely together and produced the book -The Rise of the Communicator (Green and Nickerson, 1992). But almost immediately there were some serious misgivings. It's easy to see one side and get indignant.

MSC Funding was Fortunate

Looking back, Miranda acknowledges how fortunate it was to secure MSC funding at that time. For example, in Leeds, a Post 16 programme of Deaf Awareness was funded by MSC and was delivered by Deaf people in colleges. The programme also supported the provision of jobs for Deaf people who otherwise would not have had such opportunities. Miranda's opinion of these people was very positive. The MSC funding also paid for some CSWs. In some instances the CSWs started off interpreting for the Deaf people who were delivering the Deaf awareness courses, but over time this spread into supporting Deaf students in colleges and adult education, none of which could have happened without the funding. The entire process would have taken even longer. However, at that time it meant that the whole process of delivering Deaf Awareness, creating employment for Deaf people and the evolution of the role of CSWs was possible. In Miranda's view, it needed something like that, i.e. an injection of external 'pump-prime funding' leading to subsequent local authority provision.

People were beginning to realise that sign language had always been used, Miranda recalls. In FE people were using sign language in some way or other way before schools because there weren't the restrictions. In schools, pupils were often forbidden to use sign language and in many reported cases, were forced to sit on their hands to prevent them from signing to one another. As soon as a Deaf school leaver applied to go to a FE college and needed sign, colleges began to bring in people who could offer communication support. This wasn't received in the same, rather negative way that was happening in schools. The result was that good people were brought in to offer communication support to Deaf students in FE including people with Deaf members of their family or Deaf friends and those with a good FE background themselves.

At one stage, researchers from the USA visited the UK to look at what was happening with communication support for Deaf students and were absolutely appalled. They were adamant that, if students needed sign language support in schools or in college, they had an interpreter. Miranda is not sure what the USA did in terms of notetaking etc. In a sense there was a part of Miranda that supported the view that you were never going to change things properly for Deaf people so long as you went for short-term pragmatic solutions. You had to sometimes say 'No, actually, it's not the case that anything's better than nothing.' Miranda's aim was always to ensure that any job was done properly, and where it was appropriate, indicate that this was good practice. She had always been keen on trying to define what was good practice.

Miranda's work in Leeds included the CSW area. She has never felt totally comfortable with the term CSW; she feels that what person X calls a CSW, person Y calls something different. That is seen as one of the problems. Between Miranda's work in Leeds, and then in LASER (Language of Sign as an Educational Resource) and the many National Association for Tertiary Education for Deaf People (NATED) people she worked with, they did define the CSW role. They also defined the skills and the knowledge needed and what qualifications were around. It wasn't defined as Occupational Standards, but they tried to advise employers about how to deploy people. They were trying to address it recognising the expectations of Deaf people as well as those of the employer and employee. There was always the question about whether CSW was the right title for the job. Whist working at The Council for the Advancement of Communication with Deaf People (CACDP), Miranda faced the same problem, in terms of CACDP's responsibility and how to define roles.

Anxious Interpreters

Some of the anxiety around CSWs at that time was coming from another emerging role, that of the sign language interpreter. When Miranda started out there was no such profession as sign language interpreter. There were four or five people, a few of whom are still working, who were clearly interpreters. CACDP developed qualifications and people were able to train to become sign language interpreters. The fact was that there were people who were fantastically good at doing that job but other than in a few settings, there was no interpreting provision. Deaf people didn't expect to have an interpreter when they went to the doctor; there just wasn't the provision. It's difficult to believe now, but there were professionals who could sign who delivered their service through signing. There were social workers who signed and a few Teachers of the Deaf who

signed as part of their role. Some Deaf people were absolutely
fine about that. The issues which emerged around a conflict
of role when both signing and delivering a service were not of
concern at the time. Deaf people were getting access and sign
language users were receiving services which were previously
not available to them.

Chief Executive

Miranda officially became Chief Executive of CACDP on
1st January 2000, although she had been working part-time
for CACDP since mid 1999 (whilst still working full time in
Leeds!). She remembers that one of her concerns when she
took over from Stewart Simpson, was that he had, to a certain
extent, raised expectations regarding CACDP's role and CSWs.
Miranda was naturally very cautious about fulfilling promises
made by the former Chief Executive, as she feels she was more
realistic. At that time the main concern for CACDP was trying
to ensure that interpreters could continue to train, become
qualified and obtain registration. Miranda was aware of the
need to continue trying to improve the training and qualifications of CSWs, but this part of her workload had to be shelved
to allow her to concentrate on the interpreting situation. Her
belief was that by getting it right in the interpreting field, and
learning lessons from that, the same mistakes wouldn't be
repeated with the CSWs.

The main emphasis at CACDP, as far as Miranda was
concerned, focused on being recognised as an awarding body.
At that time, some of the work that CACDP was involved with
was not consistent with being an awarding body and therefore
changes had to be made. It was deemed vital not only to bring
in experts from the Deaf field, but people who knew how to
design a qualification and how to design assessments.

Miranda recalls that there were lots of mutterings going on about CACDP doing something about CSWs. Stewart Simpson had told Miranda that registration of CSWs was what was needed. However, Miranda had by now come to realise what was involved in setting up a registration system. It wasn't just a matter of passing an examination and having your name entered on a register. There was a great deal more involved than that. By joining a register there would be some sort of regulation. Miranda shudders when she remembers that time, setting up the new registration system, and working with interpreters and universities who were offering training for interpreters.

Over time CACDP came to define what Miranda began to call the 'Language Service Professionals' role which was very much consistent with CACDP's role as an awarding and registration body. Qualifications in language and communication systems with Deaf and Deafblind people were offered. Miranda considers that it was appropriate that the register should consist of people whose role was clearly to provide that.

CSW Officer Appointed

Despite her reservations, Miranda supported CSWs during her time at CACDP. She recalls that there was a CSW committee at CACDP, which CACDP funded. CACDP put money into the CSW area for little directly in return, because it was felt important to provide such a forum and an outlet. Miranda then subsequently appointed Wendy Martin as CSW Officer, whose job was to maintain those links. CACDP always had the CSW committee, CSWs who were also interpreters were doing sign language exams, so they were being accommodated in a way. Miranda also made clear to them what registration entailed. They were told 'you have to have National Occupational Standards (NOS)'. CACDP invested a great deal of money in the development and maintenance of the LSP registers. Although it was an income generator, it cost more to run than it generated. It was cross-subsidised by qualifications, a situation which the Board of Trustees rightly questioned. CSWs, particularly those who were interpreters as well, got involved in the registration development and came to appreciate how difficult it was going to be to set up and run a register for CSWs.

Imprecise Definition is the Barrier

Indirectly some progress towards registration did take place, Miranda feels. However, because she understands the registration system so well, she is still reluctant to give her support for a registration category for CSWs. She is still cautious about the role and feels that it is still not clear and agreed what a CSW is expected to do. Is it BSL interpreting, notetaking, lipspeaking, tutorial support, pastoral support? Is there a core role to do with education support onto which language access things are added? Miranda wanted everything defined quite precisely and saw the title of the role as, for example: CSW (BSL/English), CSW(....) depending on what the expertise was. In her opinion, people get a bit hung up on registers, thinking that if you're not a registered professional you are not good enough.

The issue of registration for CSWs is much more complicated than people realise, in Miranda's opinion. In her view, if you're going to have a register, you have to do it properly. The people on it have to pay, they have to abide by the rules, and they have to be subject to the sanctions. They also need a professional association for their support, for top-up training etc. But the role of CACDP/Signature has to be absolutely clear.

In reality, Miranda claims, the NRCPD (The National Registers for Communication Professionals working with

Deaf and Deafblind People) registers aren't legitimate registers in the true sense of the word, for example like those for nurses, doctors and social workers which are government controlled and compulsory. Apparently the Association of Sign Language Interpreters (ASLI) had wanted control of the registers. Miranda recalls thinking 'Why did I bother?' No one ever said 'Thank you for what you did on the registration system' or, 'That registration system is really good.' She is sure that the registers now are the best they can be, given that they aren't compulsory and government underwritten. But she feels that you are not going to get colleges saying 'We will only use registered CSWs' because of the reality of students arriving at college unexpectedly on the first day of term when all the support has been arranged - that is just life.

Miranda feels that it is vitally important not to lose sight of Deaf people without whom the CSWs would not have developed their skills. She recalls that CSWs always had the support of NATED and did have access to CACDP's qualifications, whereas, during her time with CACDP, there was no money to develop qualifications specifically for Deaf people. Many Deaf people were working in two languages, in TV etc, but had no qualifications or support. Thankfully the situation is slowly changing now, with Signature currently piloting a Level 6 qualification in BSL translation, aimed mainly at Deaf people.

To conclude, whilst at CACDP, Miranda put resources into many things that cost more than they delivered, but were ethically right. Part of her role wasn't just responding to the noisy people. To her, it never felt right just to be focusing exclusively on hearing people and what they wanted. Miranda states that she, personally, owes all of her sign language to Deaf people. It is important that we do not lose sight of why we do the jobs we do and to whom we owe our skills and opportunities.

Where Are You Now?

Miranda retired at the end of 2006 and spent a few years living in France, relaxing and enjoying life. Eventually the pull of home and family brought Miranda and her husband Mike back to England. They now live in Oxfordshire and are enjoying their retirement, although Miranda still likes to keep up with developments within the Deaf world.

In the Beginning: I Was There

Cath Smith

Interview: Friday 4 November 2011, Darlington

Cath's reflections predate the formal training of CSWs by some years, but are useful to set the scene and give some indication to the background surrounding the emergence of Communication Support Workers (CSWs) in the late 1980s.

In 1971 Cath qualified as a social worker, having trained in Manchester. Her training included a 'Deaf Option' which she and two other students signed up for, which involved the basics to develop skills to work with Deaf people. Later, during the period 1972-1973 Cath took the Polytechnic of North London course leading to qualification as Social Worker for the Deaf which was reduced to two terms because of the above. It was a small course of nine students and she shared accommodation with two other students from the course, Mary Fielder and Sue Jones in North London. Post qualification she returned to Chester and North Wales Voluntary Society for the Deaf. As in most Deaf services at the time, many of the staff were children of Deaf parents with British Sign Language (BSL) as a first language and the service was very much the 'old school' style Deaf focus approach.

In 1973 Cath moved to the Northeast. She contacted three local authorities, seeking work as a social worker for the Deaf. The local authorities were: Durham, Newcastle and Teesside. Newcastle and Teesside both responded, but at interview in Newcastle it became clear that the team wanted to fill the role with a female worker specifically because of hospital appointments with women, whereas Teesside were offering a wider role that could be developed county-wide at Senior Social Worker grade and this was the option she took.

Cath had worked with Robin Caley in Chester and he had also previously worked for Teesside and provided a link to the process of a move to a direct local authority service. Cath worked for Teesside local authority for five years before moving on.

The Return of the Mission

Cath remembers that the local authority had a very poor understanding of how the Deaf Community functioned and the need for community involvement which was very different from the 'social work' model that the service was determined to follow. She recalls that she published an article for Deafness Magazine entitled 'The Return of the Mission?' since Mission Statements had suddenly become very popular. This was an attempt to draw attention to the fact that services were falling very short of Deaf people's needs within the community. The drive for the move away from the older Voluntary Society and 'Deaf Mission' approach had been very much orchestrated by hearing professionals, not Deaf led, and had in many ways 'thrown the baby out with the bath water'.

The Move into Education

Late in 1979 Cath was contacted by Terry Morris, who was the new Head Teacher of Beverley School for the Deaf, Middlesbrough. At that time, like most other Deaf schools in this country, the school used the oral method of educating Deaf children. Terry Morris brought with him the move towards a bilingual approach and was looking for someone to introduce signing into the school - this was long before Deaf people were involved or even consulted on BSL teaching (a term which was also not yet coined).

Cath was delighted at this change in the school's policy and accepted the post of unqualified supply teacher. At that time Cath could use BSL, but had limited school vocabulary. She instinctively knew that she had to do something about this. After doing some research and making enquiries, Cath and Terry Morris went to Moray House in Edinburgh and had a meeting with Martin Colville and Lillian Lawson. Schools in Scotland had been using fingerspelling and signing for some time, and it made sense to link into this. The team at Moray House gave help with sign vocabulary which was filmed onto video to take back to Middlesbrough.

BSL Teacher

Cath led classes in BSL in four districts of Teesside for teachers and parents of Deaf children. It is important to remember that there were no trained Deaf tutors to teach BSL. This situation was to change some years later.

Miranda Pickersgill had worked at Beverley School as a Teacher of the Deaf (ToD) but had left before Cath joined the staff. She had already altered her views away from oralism to sign language following her contact and involvement with the adult Deaf community through the British Deaf Association (BDA) and become passionate about introducing sign into education for Deaf children. She and Cath had worked together and jointly took the pupils on a week's holiday during the summer break when Cath was still a social worker.

In 1985 Cath and Terry produced the first dictionary of signs - 'Communication Link' (this was Manpower Services Commission funded). They used a team of ten people, consisting of illustrators, video technicians and a supervisor (Tony Beckett, now a BSL interpreter, was part of this team). The team were based in the attic of the old Art College in Middlesbrough. Cath later discovered that this was the former Deaf School - a real coincidence.

Terry had set up the project to develop the dictionary because no resources were available at that time to support the families and teachers using sign language. Certain factions of the Deaf world had a very negative attitude to this, since it was not Deaf-led and was regarded as a simplistic approach, but it swept the country because of the urgent need for such resources and was later updated and changed with the help of the Deaf staff who joined the school and through consultation with the Deaf community.

The British Deaf Association (BDA) published its own sign language dictionary seven years later in 1993, so in effect Communication Link had provided a much needed life-raft for many families and teachers and had supported countless Deaf children through their formative and school years.

Cath went on to write and publish other illustrated books including Signs Make Sense and Signs in Sight in which she was more able to portray her own views and understanding of how BSL worked as a language and the importance of Deaf culture.

Scant Consultation Within the Deaf Community

When asked about her memories of the unrest by social workers around the time of the introduction of the register for interpreters in the early 1980s, Cath acknowledged that she was aware of a lot of anxiety from people who had been regarded as leaders in the field who were having to go through rigorous assessment procedures and unbelievably, some were failing. One recollection of the introduction of a separate profession of interpreters is that yet again, like the move to take over the Voluntary Societies, this was a move driven by hearing professionals. There had been scant consultation within the Deaf community. Most grass-roots Deaf people were happy to continue to be supported by social workers for employment, GP and hospital appointments etc. because they (usually) had trust and confidence in the social worker that they had perhaps known for most of their life; they felt comfortable even though impartiality could sometimes be an issue.

Separate Professions was Assumed as Right

In connection with the introduction of communication support workers, Cath recalls a conference where the speakers appeared to take it for granted that the move towards separate professions of interpreters and communicators was unquestionably right. However a study at that time (which was also quoted at the conference) showed that 74% of Deaf people questioned said they preferred social workers to fulfill this function.

The fight for Deaf people to be acknowledged as the only ones appropriate for teaching BSL was widely supported at that time, but on one tutor training weekend at Durham University, one of the language professors was asked if he agreed that only Deaf people should teach BSL. The reply was a definite 'No'. The important factors he listed were the ability and skill of the teacher concerned and that being a first language user was no guarantee of teaching ability - whether teaching French, Chinese or BSL. Hearing or Deaf people who are skilled in the language and competent at teaching make the best teachers and non Deaf people should not be excluded. This was not taken very well by the Deaf members of the audience at the time, who were adamant that BSL should be taught by Deaf people - but at the same time, the stance is understandable in view of the generations of oppression that Deaf people have experienced.

Where Are You Now?

Cath still lives in Stockton on Tees and continues to produce sign graphics, books and teaching materials for BSL that are widely used and valued by Deaf and hearing teachers.

In the Beginning: I Was There

Peter Llewellyn-Jones

Interview: Saturday 14 January 2012, Lincolnshire

We interviewed Peter one evening at his home, sipping cups of tea, watched by 'One-Eye' his adopted cat, and he started by explaining how he got into the Deaf world. He explained that when he was a boy he didn't know anyone who was Deaf. He left school in 1966-7, went through a drama course in 1968, and in 1969 went to work for a voluntary organisation called Taskforce in Islington, London. There he came across one Deaf person but it didn't really make too much of an impact. He remembers around late 1978 or early 1979 going to the RNID (later becoming Action on Hearing Loss) for a meeting with Harry Jones who informed him about opportunities working with Deaf people. He was interested but because there was no subsequent contact he forgot all about it.

Hitch-hiking through Denmark

It was around one year later when Peter was hitch-hiking round Denmark, that unbeknown to him, his father was busy finding a job for his wayward son. Peter's father was a church of England vicar in Berkhamsted, and while reading the local diocese magazine he spotted a job for his son. It was for a trainee Welfare Officer for the Deaf in the St Albans diocese. He was convinced that Peter would turn out to be a wastrel so he applied for the job without asking him. Peter was furious for a while, but in the cold light of day he considered his financial situation (he was absolutely broke) so he decided to attend the interview.

Peter also applied for a job working with boats. This was for an outboard engine maintenance post for the 'Missionary to the Solomon Islands' society. He was offered that job because he had some experience of tuning and racing motorbikes. He was considering it, but had a phobia about injections so backed out. It seemed fortuitous that he was destined to work with Deaf people although he had never really met any. There was vague interest, but he knew nothing about sign language. Peter therefore found himself in the St Albans Association for the Deaf, employed as a trainee. It was one of the traditional organisations that employed people who were then called 'welfare officers'.

At that time nearly all the traditional voluntary organisations were part of a network that was responsible for training the next generation of welfare officers. It meant that part of the job involved a two or three year part-time training course, where trainees worked in the centres for the Deaf, went to week-long lecture sessions in London, plus attended local colleges. The two year option was the Certificate in Deaf Welfare, and the three year was the Diploma. That was why interpreters were called DWEBs, which was the acronym for the Deaf Welfare Examination Board, that was established in 1928 and, in the early-mid 60s even had its own college in London.

Social Workers were the Interpreters

It was very much the norm that welfare/social workers were interpreting, so right from the start Peter needed to learn sign language very, very quickly. He was based in Deaf Clubs at least three nights a week so was exposed to sign language all the time. There were no sign language classes in those days so the way to learn was working with Deaf people. Peter's employer was Tom Wordley, who was very pro-active. His view was that if Peter was going to be trained properly he needed a broad training. He sent Peter on British Deaf and Dumb Association (BDDA) courses (the word 'dumb' wasn't dropped until a few years later, Peter thinks in 1971 or 1972). Peter attended their summer schools and outdoor adventure courses, plus he was expected to attend the Deaf club that was run by the St Albans Diocesan Association in Watford. They had branches in Leighton Buzzard, Luton and Bedford and so Peter attended these nearly every night of the week. He was immersed in a signing community, mixing with young and old Deaf people, so he learned to sign very quickly and started doing the occasional interpreting jobs even as a trainee.

After about a year Peter was asked to stand in for an interpreter who was ill, and duly interpreted a BDDA course in Slough. Under the strength of that the BDDA put him on their interpreting list and he was invited to interpret all the their National events. Peter believes it was around 1969-70 when it dawned on him that interpreting was what he really enjoyed. He went home thinking, "Yep, that was great." He realised that he enjoyed interpreting more than the welfare or the social work. He qualified as an interpreter in 1972 after training for three years.

Although he was training in St. Albans, demand for Peter's interpreting work became popular thanks to the BDDA. Before he became fully qualified he was already interpreting in the BDDA congresses and the major national meetings such as the RNID (Royal National Institute for the Deaf) conferences. After qualifying in 1972 Peter went to work full time for the BDDA (by then the BDA) and was with them for about five years.

An opportunity arose in 1977 for him to become Principal of

the Bristol Centre for the Deaf. Since 1976, Peter had been a
key member of the BDA's Standing Conference on Interpreter
Training and, through moving to Bristol, he met Dr Jim Kyle,
a research psychologist at Bristol University, who had been a
member of Dr Reuben Conrad's research team that led to the
publication of the most comprehensive study of the language
abilities of Deaf school leavers, 'The Deaf Schoolchild' (1979).
They decided that research was needed into interpreting
so Peter wrote a proposal, jointly with Jim Kyle. They won
funding for three years' research into two strands: one was
learning BSL and the other was interpreting. The team was
based in the School of Education Postgraduate Research Unit
and as part of the project experimented with teaching elements
of sign language to classes in an attempt to identify different
methods. Peter then spent the next three years as a full-time
university researcher, experimenting with interpreting teaching
methods and presenting conference papers on their findings.

Interpreter Training

During research the Bristol team considered how spoken
language interpreters were trained. The nearest training course
was held at the University of Bath, so Peter went along and
observed some classes. The team started considering whether
the process of interpreting was similar if not the same as spoken
language interpreting, so Peter did a lot of work at the university on psychological models and the process of interpreting.
By the time the project finished in the early 1980's there was
a move to offer advanced training to interpreters. At that time
there was no national mapping for qualifications. Around
1980 the RNID advertised a short course in advanced interpreting run by Percy Corfmat, one of the country's best known
interpreters, who has been long deceased. That was a one-off

course. Bristol then began to develop some short courses in interpreting but there was nothing formalised at university level, and National Vocational Qualifications (NVQs) were to come later. There were no formalised qualifications. The qualified interpreters were welfare officers who had been assessed in interpreting as part of the traditional DWEB qualification so at least they had been assessed. During the late 1970s the BDA was considering how to assess interpreters with a view to setting up a register.

Peter left Bristol in 1981 and went back to the BDA to lead the communicating and interpreting services for the BDA. This lasted for a short time because he was recruited to Tyne Tees television to help develop a current affairs programme called 'Listening Eye'. In 1987 he took a job in London at the RNID as the joint head of the Department of Human Communication with Ann Parker. This was because of his experience at Bristol, his research on spoken language interpreters and his campaigning to get interpreting recognised at university level. Prior to this, in 1986 he had informally met with like-minded people and started an embryonic association which became the Association of Sign Language Interpreters (ASLI) in 1987 - the first formal meetings being held in the Magic Circle, which was housed in the basement of the RNIDs building in Gower Street.

Campaigning and Recognition

Peter led a move towards trying to get university recognition for interpreting, and there followed campaigning to raise the recognition of BSL. The aim was to get BSL recognised, then interpreter training, mirroring spoken language interpreter training at university level – that was the big push.

While Peter was at the RNID he became aware of the Manpower Services Commission (MSC) Project and the setting up of a CSW course. He was invited to give talks on those early courses in Coventry at the Deaf Club, and he was happy to oblige, although he never went to Bournville College. Peter got involved with mixed feelings because his department at the RNID was focused on interpreter training and recognition at university level. They were annoyed at the new CSW initiative because the involvement of the MSC meant that people were taken off the unemployment register – it meant that sign language interpreting was somehow devalued – anybody could do it. Peter and his circle were attempting to show that actually, people needed skills and a broad education. The CSW initiative seemed to be the opposite of what they had been campaigning for – it was deemed to be a lower form of interpreting. That is why there was a lot of resistance from those who said that interpreters needed a more academic training.

Vocal against the CSW initiative

Peter personally felt this resistance also, although he did understand that 'you have to cut your cloth according to the width'. That is why Peter is not a fan of funded projects because there is always a compromise: people end up not doing what they want, but rather, they do what the money allows them to do. Peter admits that he was probably one of the most vocal against the CSW initiative. Having said that, he happily made guest appearances on the CSW training courses because his view was, that if people were needed to work with Deaf people, they should be trained and be as highly skilled as possible. It is interesting to note that some of the students who were on the initial CSW course have ended up working with Peter's company, SLI. Peter comments that they turned out to be incredibly bright people and highly skilled. So over the last twenty years or more, Peter has been very pro-active in saying that he personally values the work that CSWs do as equally as he does interpreters. He is amused at the conflict between the stereotypical interpreter and the stereotypical CSW. He believes that the work that most CSWs do is much more about proper interpreting than the work of some who call themselves interpreters, because the latter view themselves as not being active participants. They say, "I'm here and I do my job and go away again" and "My role boundaries don't allow me to do such and such", which to Peter's view is 'nonsense dreamt-up sign language interpreting, that no spoken language interpreters would subscribe to'. Spoken language community interpreters identify much more with the work that CSWs do. In other words, the CSW's and the interpreter's collective role is to make the communication event successful. So Peter has more time for skilled CSWs than for some of the very pompous interpreters who are mistaken in thinking they know what the role of an interpreter is. In fact he holds them responsible for preventing the profession from developing over the years. He has become a supporter of the CSW role.

The First ASLI Meeting

We asked Peter about the first ASLI meeting, at the Magic Circle in Gower Street. Peter explained that it wasn't the first, because groups of colleagues had met informally in the Tyne Tees offices in London – because he was working for them at the time, he had free use of their offices for the meetings. They also ran a two day course in Bedfordshire, where spoken language interpreters presented about their work. Peter, Liz Gibson and others provided responses to their talks, as a forum to discover in what respect spoken language interpreting equated to sign language interpreting, and what the implications were. The original aim of ASLI was to engender thinking, as a forum for interpreting. Peter mused that it was a response to CACDP (later becoming Signature), which had turned out not to be a forum for interpreting. The whole point of setting up a register from the BDA's point of view was to have an organisation that interpreters belonged to that was self-regulating but where interpreting could be advanced, loosely based on the RID model in North America, run by interpreters. Peter used the word 'nicked' because he considers that the register was taken over by CACDP and became administered by an organisation where no one knew anything about interpreting. There were two representatives from each of the member organisations but none of them was interpreting-specific. Around 1986 many interpreters were frustrated with not having a forum for interpreters, so Peter started making phone calls to friends with the aim of creating an interpreter organisation. The initial meetings were in the Tyne Tees office with people like Clark Denmark, possibly Paddy Ladd (if Peter's memory serves him well) but certainly Dot Miles, John Lee, Alan Haythornthwaite and Linda Richards. It was a group of the old regulars who, in the Summer of 1987 held the first big AGM that was open to everybody, in the Magic Circle. Marina MacIntyre visited from the States for that first big meeting.

The First Item on the Agenda

The ASLI website shows the minutes for that first meeting. The very first item was 'Communication support workers' and the second was 'The importance to include communicators within ASLI'. Peter remembers the discussion well because it was about who could be members of ASLI. Should it be limited to those people who called themselves interpreters, or also those who called themselves communicators, or CSWs? Peter can't recall which side he voted on, although he seems to remember he was in favour of including CSWs because he saw ASLI as a discussion forum, not a register. The aim was not to create a political or campaigning body, but rather, a forum for interpreters to discuss interpreting. Peter has always been inclusive in his approach but he remembers that it was a hot potato from the very start. The discussion ranged around whether, if CSWs were included, they should have voting rights with level parity or less. Peter's view was that they should. After all, the interpreters weren't going into colleges. It wasn't part of their role because all their time was taken up dashing around doing community interpreting. No interpreters were going into colleges, certainly none regularly. No one was doing it until CSWs started – there was a big gap in education. Deaf people needed access to colleges. Peter holds to the old BDA ethos (from the 1970's and well into the 80's) which was very much about developing communicating opportunities for Deaf people. Allen Hayhurst, the General Secretary of the BDA in 1970s made the case that Deaf people didn't need the 'new breed' of social workers, but rather, they needed access. The need was to develop interpreting services for Deaf people to have access. That was very much a BDA initiative backed up by Karl Kirschner, from the American RID, who attended the BDA conference in Oxford in 1976. That's where the move to set up a British register started. That was very much the focus of a BDA three year project at that time, to campaign for Deaf people to have access to communication – that was the whole point.

We discussed the present day rift between CSWs and interpreters, and Peter commented that in his view it is foolish if interpreters and CSWs don't work closely together. They have separate organisations because their remits and employment conditions are clearly very different – a CSW working for a college or a school is bound by the employment conditions with less pay than interpreters and without necessarily the variety of work that interpreters have. Although, Peter thought for a moment and said that actually, interpreting is changing in that respect, with less variety of work. He commented that present-day interpreters doing Access to Work assignments and designated interpreting aren't getting the variety that was traditionally associated with community interpreting. The same applies for court interpreting, because a great many interpreters, Peter included, won't work with some interpreting agencies and won't support the Ministry of Justice contracts. The old days when the sign language interpreter had all that variety of interpreting (arriving, interpreting and then leaving) are disappearing fast, and in its place is designated interpreting, or specialisms.

Another recent shift is that there is great pressure on interpreters to reduce their rates. In Peter's view they have been artificially high for far too long, so the pendulum is swinging which is positive. The interpreters may complain about it, but the artificially high charges have actually restricted Deaf people from access because people haven't been able to afford to bring in qualified interpreters. That was one of the negative impacts of the 'professionalisation' of interpreting. On the other hand, Peter considers that CSWs are doing sterling work, very often doing the most difficult form of interpreting. They are expected to do simultaneous interpreting in lectures on technical topics that they may not particularly be experts in – that would be testing for any qualified interpreter. He thinks CSW skills need to be as high as they can possibly be.

The Breadth of the CSW Role

Peter has no argument at all with the breadth of role that the CSW has because he argues that any competent interpreter needs that breadth of role also. Any interpreter who refuses to be flexible in what they do, Peter thinks, is outdated because that is not what employers require from people in any job these days. Employers want flexibility from all members of staff. There is no employment where staff are told "You will only do what you are qualified to do". In any institution, the qualifications of staff are largely irrelevant because everyone works as a team. The notion that for ethical reasons, interpreters shouldn't do what they are not qualified to do is pure fantasy and nonsense.

Peter doesn't see a big difference between the work of CSWs and interpreters – the major difference is in employment tradition and employment terms and conditions. Interpreters need to get more realistic about the flexibility they need which is much more akin to CSWs, and CSWs need to get their act together in terms of pushing for higher level qualifications. Peter is very critical of the new Signature CSW qualification because he feels its aim is too low. The schools and colleges will not offer the wages to attract the better-educated people, so they will not have the status within education. Peter feels it is a vicious circle because the CSW course is expensive, but the newly qualified CSWs will be paid nothing more than classroom assistants. Peter's view is that a political shift is required – possibly one led by the Department of Education, that should start by recognising the skills and the needs of Deaf students, then look at the staff required to support them. His view is that if a higher level of CSW training is available, interpreters would have to take stock and say "Well actually these people are as well trained and qualified as we are." That is Peter's vision for the future.

Peter's other vision is to move interpreters away from the old fashioned idea that interpreting is a restricted role, to move away from unintelligent ideas of ethics and codes of conduct etc. Interpreters should move away from those restrictive perceptions and start to look honestly at what they are required to do. In Peter's view, the role that some interpreters mistakenly have is not the role that Deaf people want. What Peter aims to do through training and academic papers and books at the moment is to educate interpreters about what they should be doing. A few years ago Peter did some consultancy work for a London borough's occupational therapy department. They said that they preferred to use CSWs because interpreters weren't flexible enough. It's a fact of life that employers don't recruit people who are not flexible.

Recognition for CSWs

Peter wants to see more recognition for CSWs, and more opportunities for them to get higher levels of training. Recently he attempted to achieve this at Leeds University and moved towards validation with a postgraduate certificate in education and communication support. Then at the last minute it was shelved because Signature announced the intention to bring out a new qualification for CSWs based on the National Occupation Standards for Learning Support Assistants. There was no point developing a course when it wasn't known whether it would be recognised. Peter asked us to put it on the record that he believes Signature and the NRCDP are responsible for holding the field back at least twenty years with its recent policies. He believes we should be looking forward, encouraging more training at university level because that engenders respect from employers and other stakeholders.

Peter wants people to accept that the CSW role is a specialist role that interpreters should be working in. He believes that it should be recognised, because CSWs perform very complex interpreting tasks, particularly for Deaf children and young people, and that there is no excuse for not recognising or valuing the role as equal to interpreters.

Peter commented that public service interpreting is beginning to be recognised at universities. The Higher Education Funding Council of England (HEFCE) recently announced a twenty thousand pound research project to look at opportunities to train public service interpreters in universities, because traditionally that has always been the case – interpreters were trained at universities – but public service interpreters had to make do with evening classes here and there. There was no real formalised training for them. That is now changing because it is beginning to be recognised that public service interpreters need exceptionally advanced and broader skills because they have to deal with all sorts of people with different vulnerabilities and complex needs. That is exactly the same as the CSW role, so we should be getting the CSW role together with the community interpreting role, into university level. Peter strongly believes that must be the next thrust.

Where Are You Now?

Peter resigned from his post as a senior teaching fellow at Leeds University at the end of December 2011. However the university asked him to continue teaching for a further semester, until the end of May 2012. Peter is busy trying to develop a raft of new courses for his training organisation Sign Languages International (SLI) because he wants to develop SLI more. He feels his departure from Leeds was well overdue, partly because he went there for two years but stayed for nearly nine. He has learned a massive amount from it but because of the government change of policy on higher education, the chances of any innovation in higher education is minimal for the next few years and he doesn't feel he has many years left. He is in his sixties so he feels that if he is going to be innovative still he needs to be in an arena where innovation is allowed. He believes the university system won't be that arena for some three, four, five years until the funding dust settles, so he deliberately pulled out of Leeds university. He is still teaching courses at UCLAN, and thinking about developments there but he is also considering developing new areas, such as moving into training the spoken language community of interpreters, which he has done recently. He taught on a ten week course in the summer of 2011 for spoken language interpreters with rare language combinations involving Kurdish, Farsi, Somalians etc. which he found fascinating. In September 2011 he taught for ten days in Beijing for the Chinese Foreign Ministry, at the Chinese foreign affairs university. He is fascinated by the training of spoken language interpreters, and has been involved in it now for five or six years. He is in talks with the Institute of Linguists, for SLI to commence training in spoken language interpreting, because he wants to broaden out. That's where Peter is now, looking at new initiatives, broadening SLI's work and giving him the chance to do a few more things before, in his own words, he 'pops his clogs'.

Would Peter Run a CSW Course?

We asked him if he would consider running a CSW course in SLI, and he replied, 'Yes, absolutely', but with the understanding that SLI will only run training that leads people somewhere and not down a dead end. It could be short-course professional development, in which case it has to be affordable and worthwhile doing, or if longer courses then there should be recognition for the qualifications that candidates achieve. Typically at SLI he has worked at university level but it doesn't have to be, because SLI has also offered NVQ assessment in the past. Peter won't accept people's money and give them a worthless piece of paper – he would never sanction that. He wouldn't want to do that himself so would not inflict it on others. If he can work out a way, he would love to train CSWs – there is no problem with that whatsoever.

We thanked Peter and One-Eye for their valuable time and completed the interview.

7

I Was There: Deaf Perspectives

Michelle Jones

Michelle Jones - Chair of NATED

Michelle is employed as a Service Team Leader for Deaf and Visually Impaired Access Service at The Manchester College. She kindly shared with us her experiences of Deafness and education from early childhood into adulthood. Michelle attended Schools for the Deaf (both day and residential), Partially Hearing Units (PHUs) and mainstream educational institutions. Therefore she has experienced a wide range of teaching methods and social situations and has been subjected to various attitudes and reactions from teachers and fellow pupils. Michelle continues her story:

I was born in Sunderland Maternity Hospital on 1st December 1974. I have been profoundly Deaf since birth. My Deafness was not confirmed until I was about two and half years old but my slow development of speech and my lack of reaction to noises had been noted by my parents from an early age. Naturally they were concerned. The diagnosis of my Deafness had been a rather slow progress. From the age of fifteen months onwards each and every occasion while attending the baby clinic my parents had expressed their anxiety to the doctors and nurses. Why was I not responding to noises or attempting 'baby talk'? Eventually routine hearing tests were carried out regularly and apparently I passed them all!! My mother was told that she was being rather over-anxious and she should not worry about my lack of speech at that particular time. In fact, according to their experience the local 'experts' suggested that some children were late talkers and that many children did not develop speech until a much later stage. Somewhat innocently my parents accepted this explanation from the professionals and assumed that surely they must be right! Moreover, apparently I appeared to be a perfectly normal, healthy and very bright child.

Profound Hearing Loss Diagnosed

However as time went by and I still wasn't making any attempt to talk, my parents became more concerned. They decided to carry out their own tests. They dropped keys behind my back; they banged drums; they shouted at me. Sometimes I appeared to respond to these sounds and at other times I did not. Perhaps sometimes I spotted what they were doing. It was all so confusing for them. I believe that things came to a head one day when my parents approached our family doctor to voice their concerns yet again. I was referred on to a hearing specialist who carried out more detailed tests to assess my degree of hearing. It was finally confirmed that I had a profound hearing loss and my parents had their suspicions confirmed.

Once my degree of Deafness had been confirmed I was provided with a large and heavy body aid and allocated two hours of speech therapy per week from a peripatetic teacher of the Deaf. The aim of this therapy was to accelerate my ability to communicate towards the perceived normal level of development, ready for starting a mainstream infants school. My mother was given advice on how to help my speech develop, and on using the apparatus with large headphones. Every afternoon, from the age of two and half, she would spend time working with me in order to develop my speech, mainly through lip-reading. I had to wear both my hearing aids at all times because, it was claimed, doing so would enable me to make use of my residual hearing, although the sounds which are received through a hearing aid are so distorted that you really can't make sense of what you are hearing.

No Benefit from Hearing Aids

It should be pointed out that most profoundly Deaf people gain no additional benefit whatsoever from wearing a hearing aid. Nevertheless, this method of teaching continued until the age of three when I started my formal education in an Infants Partially Hearing Unit (PHU). A PHU is based within a mainstream school. These units are usually sound-proof and equipped with specialised equipment to help Deaf children. Equipment includes, for example, a 'phonic ear', which is a microphone device worn by both teacher and pupil that amplifies the voice and cuts out background noise. This is known as a 'Group Aid'. The education I received was an oral one in which there was a strong emphasis on speech and lip-reading. The use of Sign Language was actively discouraged. However, at this time I really had no knowledge of sign language. My parents were both hearing and I never came into contact with any other Deaf children or adults who signed outside the PHU. It was only when I went to a boarding school for the Deaf I became aware of Deaf people who had their own language – Sign Language.

Total Communication

At the Milan Convention in 1880 hearing professionals had advocated that the oralist approach was the best method of teaching for Deaf children and that sign language was to be banned in schools. However, there had recently been a movement towards the use of Total Communication in the teaching of Deaf children using both the oral/aural approach and British Sign Language (BSL). For many Deaf children, sign language is their first language – especially if they are born to Deaf parents. Why shouldn't they be educated in their own language?

I stayed in the infant PHU until I was seven years old and although my memories of this time are now very vague. I do remember that I was the only girl out of a total of seven children, all the rest being boys whose ages varied from between three to seven years.

The next stage of my education until I was twelve years old also took place in a PHU (Junior). Part of my timetable involved integration, that is joining the 'big classroom' with my hearing peers. For the most part I felt I was left alone to work on my own in the 'big classroom' and I received little attention from the teachers. This was probably due to the fact that they had thirty other children to teach as well as me. In the PHU seven of us shared two adults, a pupil teacher ratio of 3.5 to 1. I felt that I did not learn anything under these conditions and I often spent my time reading. I could not understand what the teachers said at all and I blame this on their lack of insight and understanding of my need to maintain sight of the movement of their lips. I now realise that they were probably not prepared for teaching Deaf children and had little or no knowledge of Deafness and its problems.

It is worth noting that the formal training of communication support workers (CSWs) had not yet started during Michelle's primary education. It is well noted that the support offered to Deaf children in education at this time was very poor. Teachers of the Deaf were few and far between, so Michelle's memories are, sadly, a reflection of most Deaf children's experiences at that time.

A Talent for Swimming

I spent only a little time with PHU Teacher of the Deaf (ToD) and the other Deaf pupils, mainly because of the diverse range of ages, abilities and needs within the unit and also because we were encouraged to cope to the best of our ability in the mainstream classes. Socially I was well adjusted and partook in many outside activities, in particular swimming which I enjoyed very much indeed. I have many medals and certificates in recognition of my swimming. I also made many friends amongst my hearing peers as my speech was good enough for me to make myself understood fairly easily.

As a result, my academic progress was considered poor and by now it was time for me to begin my secondary education. My parents looked into the possibility of sending me to a small private school or a school for the Deaf. They felt I would not to be able to achieve a high level of performance or broad academic education if I was left to cope within a mainstream school. We visited St John's Residential School for the Deaf at Boston Spa and my parents were impressed with the high standard of teaching there. For my part I immediately fell in love with the school. I was struck by the warmth and politeness of the pupils and became excited about the prospect of joining the school. My parents approached our local education authority (LEA) with a view to having me educated there. However, at the time my parents had not considered the arrogance of or power of the Local Authority. My parents' request to have me educated at St John's was refused. In the LEA's opinion my needs could equally be fully met within a mainstream school. As a Deaf child, my speech was good so I was considered to be an oral success. So much for parental choice!

Parental Battles for Specialist Education

At that time in England the LEAs were under an obligation to implement 'statements' setting out the educational provision and requirement for children with special needs. My parents appealed against LEA's decision to have me educated in a mainstream school. They wanted me to be educated by specialist teachers of the Deaf so that I could have the chance to achieve my full potential. It took my Local Authority eighteen months to implement another 'statement'. After a long hard battle between both the LEA and my parents it was agreed that I could at last go to St John's where I would be taught by qualified teachers of the Deaf. I am an only child and this decision to have me educated in a Special School for the Deaf which was many miles away from home could not have been an easy decision for my parents to fight for and accept. But they were prepared to make this sacrifice in order to give me as good an education as possible and I will always be grateful to them that they made the right decision.

I spent the next six years at St John's, which is a convent school with strictly observed rules. I still have very happy memories of my time there. At St John's the teaching methods suited me as there were small classes, each with eight pupils, all the same age as me. We were taught according to our academic needs. The teachers there were able to concentrate on our particular needs which means I made rapid progress. It was an oral school and again sign language was forbidden. I enjoyed the lessons as, after years of seldom speaking up in the PHU, I was able to fully participate in class discussions. This was another aspect of the school's teaching methodology and thus speaking was encouraged in order to improve speech.

As St. John's was a small residential school, the social life revolved around the pupils. Everyone knew each other and I did make several close friendships which I still maintain even today. It was at this school that I first encountered sign language as the school catered for a variety of pupils, some with poor speech and a good command of sign language. I quickly learned how to sign but it was not a proper form of language as it was based on our own inventions. It was therefore a local dialect. We used it to ease understanding of speech but this was forbidden by the school, so we were careful not to get caught! Indeed we were sometimes punished if we were caught signing. How old fashioned that seems today!

After achieving eight GCE O-levels, I was accepted at Harrogate College to study a Business and Finance course. St John's, in conjunction with the College, were trying to establish links for Deaf students. I would still remain a boarder at St John's and I would continue to receive supplementary support from its teachers in the evening. I was seventeen at this time and armed with my experience from the sixth form, I was ready to embark on this course. I felt that being in a hearing institution would improve my communication skills and increase my confidence. The school allowed me to develop into an independent person as I had to stand on my own two feet. I felt I was able to cope with changing educational environments.

How wrong I was! The transition from school into college was very traumatic. I was expected to lip-read the tutors. I remember with horror my first morning when I walked into the classroom and found out my lecturer had a beard!! I was sitting right at the front of the classroom and he started talking. He mumbled for twenty minutes and I hadn't a clue what he was talking about! Other students started putting their hands up one after another and I didn't know why. The lecture continued and still I couldn't understand a word. I was beginning to panic whilst everyone else was scribbling furiously. I began copying from a textbook so that I looked as if I was taking notes just like everyone else. Whether the book was anything to do with the lecture I didn't know and, frankly, I didn't care. At the end of the lecture, before I could explain my difficulties, the lecturer had left the room. At lunchtime I found the refectory and my heart sank. It was huge – there seemed to be thousands of students there. I couldn't locate my other Deaf friends, who were all on different courses. I wanted someone to sit with, someone to talk to. By the end of the day I was completely demoralised. What had gone wrong? The answer is that my needs and those of other Deaf students were not understood.

Deaf Awareness training was arranged by St John's school for the tutors at the College and over a period of time things did improve a little but it turned out to be a constant battle for us Deaf students to be accepted. I managed to complete the course but I wouldn't have succeeded without the help and support of one of my teachers at St John's. Together we would 'burn the midnight oil' going over notes from my tutors and re-enforcing my work from the college.

Again, it is worth noting that, hopefully, this situation would not happen today. Usually, prior to commencing a course of further education, a disabled student would complete a

'Statement of Needs' or something similar, in which types of support would be identified, for example, a CSW, notetaker, lipreader etc. In most cases, communication support would be put in place from the start of the Deaf student's enrolment. What a difference such a system would have made to Michelle had this support been available when she attended Harrogate College.

Studies Nearer Home

After this long and difficult year I decided I wanted to return home. All my friends at school had left college but I felt the need to continue to further my education. I was lucky enough to secure a place at Gateshead College which was near to my home. There I embarked on a two year GNVQ Level 3 Business and Finance course and the Funding Council provided me with a full-time Teacher of the Deaf. My experience at Gateshead was entirely different to that at Harrogate College. Here I was given every support – the tutors were brilliant! I felt I could approach them and they were very understanding towards my Deafness. My teacher signed to me in lecturers and I enrolled onto Sign Language classes to increase my knowledge of BSL. I left Gateshead after gaining a distinction in all my modules. I wouldn't say it had been easy. Even today I find it difficult to partake fully whenever I find myself in group situations. Most people talk very fast and I can lose the thread of conversations even with my interpreter signing to me. I also find this to be true in family get-togethers.

After leaving Gateshead College I was accepted by Central Lancashire University to study a combined honours degree in Computing, Deaf Studies and Education Studies. The University is very much aware of the needs of Deaf students but I feel that some staff need more training in Deaf Awareness. I received support from a note taker, a communicator and a language support tutor full-time. I simply would not have been able to complete the course without the support of all these people.

After university, I achieved a job as a Careers Advisor at Breakthrough UK Ltd to teach hearing students in basic skills – Literacy and Numeracy. I was provided with two part time Access to Work interpreters to enable me to communicate with the hearing students. I realised I couldn't develop tutor–student relationships because of our communication differences. I left after two years and applied for a Tutor of Deaf Students role at Bolton College where I taught access to further education courses for Deaf learners. Whilst there I realised that I wanted to become a Teacher of the Deaf. I went to Leeds University to study a part- time Advanced Deaf Education course in order to become a qualified Teacher of the Deaf. Whilst there I was provided with support from a note-taker and an interpreter.

At present I work at The Manchester College as team leader for the Deaf and Visually Impaired Access Service and receive support from two part-time Access to Work interpreters and a part-time personal communication assistant. Part of my role is to ensure extensive and high quality student support services are available throughout the college. Support is matched to individual learner needs and personal targets to enable learners to access and achieve their educational aims.

I became Chair of NATED (National Association for Tertiary Education for Deaf People) in 2010 and enjoy this role very much.

To conclude, throughout my education and working life, I have received communication support from a variety of professionals: Teachers of the Deaf, notetakers, communicators and BSL interpreters. Without them I would not be where I am today.

Emma Green

Interview: Monday 23 January 2011, Coventry

We interviewed Emma at City College Coventry on Monday 23 January 2012. She is a bubbly, friendly person who greeted us with a smile and immediately put us at ease. She has a progressive hearing loss, and has used a communication support worker throughout her education and working life. She has worked in further education in Coventry since leaving university in 1998, and has been a lecturer on CSW training courses for a number of years. In 2010 she was the lead tutor on the first pilot course of the new Signature qualification for CSWs, and so has become an important part in the history of CSWs.

Emma was born in 1974 in Coventry and has lived in the area all her life. She has a Deaf mother and a hearing father. Emma went to a mainstream primary school in Coventry. Even though her mother is Deaf and Emma had a lot of hearing tests when she was younger, her hearing loss wasn't recognised until she was about five years old. The diagnosis occurred after she had suffered from mumps. At the same time new audiometers were introduced for testing hearing. So, it is unclear whether the hearing loss was there, but the technology wasn't there to identify it, or whether the mumps triggered a weakness of some sort. Emma started wearing hearing aids from the age of five. In her opinion, her hearing loss wasn't that bad at first, but it is progressive. It was very stable for most of her school career, but got progressively worse over the last fifteen or twenty years.

Emma attended mainstream primary school and does not recall experiencing any problems. She was, and still is, quite sociable and made lots of friends. When Emma was preparing for the transition into secondary education, it was decided that she wouldn't be able to attend her local secondary school because it was considered that she would struggle too much. By this point her hearing loss was getting worse, because it is a progressive condition.

Treated Differently

At the age of eleven, Emma went to Blue Coat Church of England School in Coventry, which had a hearing impaired unit. She had received some support in primary school, a Teacher for the Deaf (ToD) used to come into school once or twice a week. Emma doesn't think she had a particularly good relationship with the ToD. She hated being taken out of class; hated it with a passion, because she felt it just made her different. When Emma started secondary school, she was determined that she was not going to be part of this Partially Hearing Unit (PHU) and was just going to go into mainstream school. That determination probably lasted for about a year to eighteen months. Then reality started to bite. Emma recalls that her school year were only the second group of students to be entered for GCSEs. (General Certificate in Secondary Education). As soon as they started preparing for GCSEs, it became more and more apparent that there were gaps in their knowledge. It was at this point that Emma got pulled in to the PHU and it was fine, once she got to know everyone. It was just a big adjustment to have to make.

Deafness Studies at Bristol

In addition to achieving GCSEs, Emma also achieved 'A' levels at school. On leaving school she worked for a year in a primary school as an education assistant. Emma couldn't decide what she wanted to do. Around this time, her Teacher of the Deaf told her about a course that was being established at Bristol University, within the Centre for Deafness Studies. A new course was due to commence the following year, aimed at Deaf people who wanted to work in Deafness studies. Emma quickly decided to apply. It was to be a one year course. She was offered a place and went to Bristol to study. While she was there the university decided to develop a degree level course. Emma duly applied to continue for the full three years.

This was the first time that she had experienced sign language. Coventry was very oral. All candidates who were 'oral' Deaf were recommended to attend Bristol six weeks in advance of the course starting to learn to sign, because all of the tutors were Deaf and communicated in British Sign Language (BSL). The tutors included Clark Denmark, Rachel Sutton-Spence, Bencie Woll and Jim Kyle. Jim was hearing, but everything was delivered in sign language. Emma and other oral Deaf students took a crash-course in sign language. The experience was a complete reversal of roles for the oral Deaf students. These students used notetakers in lectures and seminars for completely the opposite reason that they had used them in class in school. Emma recalls that the experience felt very strange, but great.

After two years of study at Bristol University, Emma had completed the course. The proposed third (degree) year was never passed through senate, so all students on the course had to leave after two years. Emma then studied for a degree in Sociology and Social Policy at the University of Warwick from 1995 until 1998. She had full support there from the Student Access Support Unit (SASU). This was known as ECSTRA (see table of acronyms) when Warren Nickerson worked at Coventry College. The support was provided for all seminars, lectures and tutorials.

After she had graduated from Warwick University, SASU asked Emma if she would like to work for them. She duly started working for SASU as soon as she graduated. Emma remarked that she has never had a job interview because she has worked for the unit ever since she left university in 1998, always part time.

Work at SASU included supporting Deaf students although Emma acknowledges that she was limited in the students that she could support. The students were mainly enrolled on basic skills courses. City College Coventry hold a regular event known as Deaf Day. The focus is on improving English for Deaf students, but also includes maths and I.T. Usually between ten or twelve Deaf students attend for the full day.

She's always held pastoral tutorials for Deaf students and has always taught Deaf Awareness. After she had been working for a couple of years and achieved a teaching qualification, she joined the team delivering CSW training. Further information on Emma's involvement in delivering CSW training can be found in chapter 13 which looks in more detail at the piloting of the new CSW qualification.

In answer to the question about what she thought of the support she has received from CSWs throughout her education and working life, Emma replied 'I could never have got anywhere near as far as I have without CSWs. It would just have been too difficult. In primary school I hated the idea of being made to be different by having this person come into the classroom. I think so much has changed since then, so my points may not be valid any more. There have been examples of clashes of personality between me and CSWs but I think you are always going to get that anyway. The way that SASU dealt with it when I was at university was just amazing. You always try to keep the CSW for continuity for knowledge and background. But these things happen. You can't always get on with everybody. But apart from that, I wouldn't be without the support. The support I had from Jane (Blundell) at Warwick

University was invaluable. I couldn't have done it without her. We got on really well and have become firm friends and colleagues. We taught the CSW course together and are friends outside of college too.'

Where Are You Now?

Emma is happily married with three young children - all Deaf. She still works for SASU. She underwent a cochlear implant in July 2011 and has found the difference it has made quite amazing. At the start, she kept asking what certain sounds and noises were. There was so much that she didn't recognise - she had to learn what these new sound were - the sound of the leather seats in the car against her clothing. The noise of her charm bracelet rattling almost drove her mad until she realised what it was. Emma admits that it's all been very strange.

However, adjusting to new sounds has been easier to get used to than she had expected. She claims that everything is a lot clearer for her now and that her confidence has increased.

She has now applied for teacher training and hopes to work in primary schools and eventually become a Teacher for the Deaf. Emma admits that this is something she would never have had the confidence to do before she had the cochlear implant.

Judith Collins

Teaching Fellow, School of Modern Languages and Cultures, Durham University.

Interview: Wednesday 16 November 2011, Durham

I was employed as a Deaf Instructor (DI) in a mainstream schools service in Leeds from 1987-1991. In 1987 the Local Education Authority (LEA) was the first to implement a Bi-Lingual Education Policy with Deaf children who prefer to use sign language. My role involved working with ethnic minorities within the Deaf and Hearing Impaired Service. In my four years I worked with the university playgroup with very young children, nursery, primary and middle schools. I was also involved with the Peripatetic teachers for home visits and a Family Support Group. During this time I was involved in research with Rob Baker from Leeds University into British Sign Language and the education of Deaf children.

Experience Working with Educational Interpreters

The bilingual education policy in Leeds called for the use of Deaf instructors and BSL/English interpreters. Deaf instructors worked alongside interpreters within the mainstream setting. Interpreters in this context were referred to as Educational Interpreters (EI) as they mainly worked in a specialist educational setting although this title was not formally recognised. It was a new area at the time.

The EI was employed to interpret at morning assemblies, in classrooms, family support groups, teacher training, staff meetings, hand over meetings and parents evenings. The EI followed the professional Code of Ethics for interpreters.

The use of Deaf instructors and interpreters enabled children to access the full range of curriculum subjects and promoted positive Deaf role models and native language models. This approach underpinned the values associated with a bilingual education policy. Employing DIs working alongside EI meant the latter was not expected to fulfil a support teaching role.

The role of the educational interpreter was continually debated within the service and eventually because of our experience of children needing teaching support it was decided the Service also needed people in the role of Support Teacher and the title would be communication support worker (CSW). It is important to remember that this was CSW as an educational support role and it was separated from that of an interpreter. CSWs had an educational role alongside teachers and Deaf Instructors. Interpreters were also employed as interpreters. If an Interpreter was in a class it was expected the person was there for the role of interpreting and not support teaching. The needs of children in particular classes were decided by pre-class planning. A number of years later the Association of Sign Language Interpreters (ASLI) produced Guidelines for Interpreters Working in Educational Settings.

DWP Report

Later, at Durham University in 2002, with Richard Brown and David Brien, I was Deaf researcher for the in-house research report, funded by the Department of Work and Pensions, The Organisation and Provision of British Sign Language/English Interpreters in England, Scotland and Wales. Deaf people's feedback was gleaned formally through one to one and public consultations and is highlighted throughout the report. Section 5.2.5.9 of the report covers CSWs and is worth quoting in full:

communication support workers engaged in interpreting.
Communication support workers are usually employed in educational settings to provide a range of services to Deaf students. Their responsibilities may include interpreting, as well as note-taking and one-to-one tutorials with Deaf students. Considerable criticism was expressed by Deaf people at the public meetings of people with Stage I and Stage II BSL qualifications being employed in these posts and, in addition, that they were being expected to interpret within the college in which they were employed. In the view of the Deaf people who raised this issue, these qualifications do not equip **communication support workers** to be able to communicate to the standard required to support Deaf students in educational settings. They argued that they were in no position to provide interpreting services in educational or any other setting. (For a discussion of the role of **communication support workers** see CACDP, 2001b; Harrington 2001; Kernoff 2001.)

Some Deaf people therefore suggested that there was need to clarify the role of **communication support workers** and, in particular, their role in relation to interpreters. A number of Deaf people expressed concern that the term 'educational interpreters' was being used to describe **communication support workers**. They felt this title was misleading and should not be used.

Recipients of both Access to Work and the Student Disability Allowance provided examples of people with Stage II BSL qualifications being recommended by Access to Work administrators and student disability advisors as appropriate persons to provide interpreting services. It was unclear to them whether this was done out of ignorance of the difference between BSL/English interpreting qualifications and the BSL language qualifications or an attempt to save money.

A version of the above report was also published in Deaf Worlds: International Journal of Deaf studies; Volume 20, issue 1, 2004. Recommendation 11.1 to 11.6 clearly puts forward the need to define the role of Communication Support Workers in relation to other professionals working in educational settings. Such clarification is important and applies in other settings too.

A PowerPoint of a presentation I made to the ACSW Conference in 2007 can be seen on-line: www.dur.ac.uk/ j.m.collins/whatisacsw.html.

Over recent years there have been ongoing email debates from subscribers to the email group E-newsli (largely professional interpreter subscribers) regarding the role and qualifications of CSWs.

The role of a support worker in education deemed only as 'communication' has always been problematic. It has clearly always been about an educational support function that is expected to include providing instruction, advice and guidance, for Deaf children and students.

A CSW is required to provide a wide range of general support to Deaf students. They are required to have CSW qualifications and hopefully a high level of fluency in both BSL and English. In essence this is a Support Tutor role supporting with English and other subjects and giving advice and guidance.

It is clearly also a role that is different from that of qualified interpreter responsibilities. Interpreters are not expected to provide instruction, advice and guidance. It is a different matter than CSWs 'simply' becoming qualified to interpret. Yet I see this is often proposed as a 'solution' to the problem and often by qualified interpreters. It shows to me either (a) some interpreters are undermining their professional role as interpreters or (b) sometimes a person is fulfilling two different roles at different times. The former is clearly a problem, the latter may perhaps be carried out responsibly in some organisational settings.

It is my professional opinion from experience of education at all levels and from many years of teaching interpreters that the role title of 'CSW' should be dropped and changed to Support Tutors (for Deaf students). They need skills and knowledge of BSL and of other ways of communicating and they also need skills and knowledge of teaching. The Support Teacher needs advanced level fluency in BSL (higher than BSL Level 2). This needs to be combined with the Post Graduate Certificate in Education.

Important decisions need to be made outside the classroom, before any class takes place as to the type of educational support that will be needed in the class: a Support Tutor (for Deaf students) or an interpreter (who will function as an interpreter with the student participating independently in class alongside other students).

8

Recent View

Jim Edwards

Interview 22nd November 2011, Durham

We met up with Jim Edwards, Chief Executive of Signature, and conducted an interview in his office in Durham. To begin, we asked for his thoughts on the role of CSWs. Our further questions are indicated in italics.

I will reply chronologically. I joined Signature in 2007 and one of the initial conversations I had with the Director of Qualifications, Cathy Barnes, was to ascertain whether there was a qualification for educational **communication support workers** (CSWs). At that stage we knew that Edexcel had a qualification but we weren't sure whether it was being taught, if it was being used, or how active and up-to-date it was. Then we commenced a dialogue with Edexcel and asked if they wanted to refresh the qualification and if they were interested in working with us. That was probably the beginning of the process. Previously Cathy had a number of conversations with Edexcel probably over a couple of years which didn't seem to move the issue forward. The reason may have been because Edexcel didn't want to relinquish it. We also thought there might well be a need, but there will also be a cost involved for us to do it.

I-Sign Partnership

We were then put into a partnership, or became part of a partnership for the I-Sign Project. I-Sign was a government funded project by what was then the Department for Children Schools and Families (DCSF). It was a two year project which started in 2009. The I-Sign Project was about improving the children's workforce (people working with Deaf children) and particularly to improve their skills in communicating with Deaf children. So, an obvious issue to consider was an ECSW (Educational Communication Support Worker) qualification for people working in the children's workforce. So we said we would develop a qualification in that area. That was funded by the DCSF. As we broke into that piece of work it became clear, when considering the education workforce from childhood through to adulthood, that we needed two qualifications not one: One to work with pre-16s and another to work with post-16s in further and higher education. Although the qualification content would be different, that was a separate matter. However, we knew that the sector skills workforces for both sectors were, and still are, different. The Teachers Development Agency (TDA) looked after those under 16, and Lifelong Learning UK (LLUK) looked after post 16. So, Cathy and other members of the team commenced a discussion, starting with LLUK, because they were looking to establish Learning Support Worker (Practitioner) standards. The door was (sort of) open to work with them, but the TDA door wasn't open because they had no immediate plans to do anything for Learning Support Workers, working in the classroom as support assistants. So we had to make a choice. Even though the I-Sign Project would have preferred us to work with the child (under 16) workforce, we knew that the opportunity to do it, to get it done, was with the adult workforce - the Post 16 workforce. We started on that journey by employing Maria Bailey as a consultant, on a part-time basis to help develop a qualification for ECSWs who were working in FE. So I think that is probably the context and the background.

Jim was asked to clarify, from becoming Chief Executive on 1 January 2007 until the I-Sign Project in 2009, what dialogue was had with Edexcel.

Cathy had had the occasional email correspondence with Edexcel. There were two main issues. One issue was that we would have to equip ourselves to work with another sector skills body (up until that point we had only worked with the languages sector skills body). So this meant us broadening our footprint, which wasn't a bad thing to do in itself. The second issue was that we would be in competition with Edexcel, which we were reluctant to do. So, we wanted to be sure that Edexcel weren't going to develop it any further. When it became apparent that they weren't that keen (even when we were writing the bid for I-Sign, we weren't sure whether we would do it on our own or with Edexcel) the way ahead was much clearer. Later it became apparent that it would be more efficient to do it ourselves anyway.

We asked Jim to comment on whether he had any dealings with CSWs, and if he was aware of the role, prior to becoming Chief Executive at Signature.

Yes, I was certainly aware of the role. I'd run several projects around developing sign language skills within Wales, and in those projects, I got close to three or four colleges who were, from my point of view, looking at how they could teach Level 3 and above British Sign Language skills. But actually, one of their interests (as colleges providing opportunities for deaf learners to access FE education) was to find out what skills CSWs needed. In fact one of the colleges – Barry College in South Wales – or at least my contact there, was involved in running the Edexcel programme at one stage, or at least had worked with the National Association for Tertiary Education for Deaf people (NATED). I think she was either secretary, or an official within NATED at one stage - and she and I had spoken about the fact that there was this Edexcel qualification and this is what it did. I remember her saying then that it had been around for a long time. It hadn't been refreshed actually. I don't know when it was last refreshed by Edexcel, but I had the sense that it was some years ago. So, whatever was around in 2007, I suspect was already quite dated.

CSW Registration

We commented that Stewart Simpson, a former Chief Executive of Signature, wrote in his book, regretting that he did not manage to ensure registration for CSWs. We asked Jim if this was something that he had been aware of, and if any progress had been made towards registration.

I know that there is a call for CSWs to register and, in fairness, I would now push that question back to the NRCPD (The National Registers of Communication Professionals working with Deaf and Deafblind People). Although Signature is the holding company for the NRCPD, that sort of policy decision very much lies with them. We have had discussions over the last three years about registration for CSWs. But we needed clarity on qualifications to start with; and having got that, then the question was 'Which is more important, a registration category or a skill that you hope someone will acquire?' Let me explain it another way. You know that we register people as interpreters etc, so, they are not domain specific. One of the options being considered at one stage was to give an opportunity for an interpreter to say 'I want a domain specific registration - e.g. for working in education.' Now, we know that the CSW role is actually very different to that of an interpreter, so you therefore have the situation of asking for registration of a role of a communication professional that is slightly different to the other roles that we have.

If CSWs were to register, I suppose we would have to ask, in terms of communication, what level of BSL would they require, or what level of other communication skill - deafblind, note-taking or whatever. Then you would have to say - we require it as a prerequisite that they have a CSW qualification. I'm not sure that it's ever got out of that sort of mush where it becomes clear whether it is a registration category or a skill. And I don't know the answer. Should it be a registration category? As part of I-Sign we had a long discussion with the Department for Education (as it was then) and all the partners and the steering group of I-Sign were saying very clearly 'If someone was working in, as it was then, an adult setting, we would want them to have the ECSW qualification, to work as a **communication support worker** and, if they were working with a BSL user, a minimum of Level 3'. But that's never been turned into a requirement. I suppose one of the questions is if the NRCPD regard a Level 3 requirement as making it eligible for registration? At least it shifts the industry along a bit. At that stage we were hoping that the Department for Education would be more explicit about what it thought the requirements were.

That's sort of, a bit, where it's stuck, I think. The Department of Education isn't declaring its hand too strongly. We are in a climate where government will seek not to regulate; seek not to specify standards, and will always want to leave that decision to the local authorities, local providers. So, I suppose the question is, in that context, would the NRCPD take a view to register ECSWs now when, actually, three years ago it wouldn't have done? It would have just kept pushing it to be recognised by mainstream organisations.

Registration Costs Prohibitive?

We made the point that during the research phase of the CSW qualification, employers had reported that they had no clue who they were employing. At least with a registration category, they would know, just as with people looking for interpreters. Also, there may be a danger that the CSW role becomes too complicated if we view it in terms of communication methods, and if so, a multi-faceted layer within the category would be required. Maybe the costs to administer such a category would be prohibitive.

The registration category wouldn't, in itself, be an enormous expense to set up. We have just consulted on a number of facets of registration, for example, CRB (Criminal Records Bureau - commonly known as the 'Police Check'); PII (Professional Indemnity Insurance); Introduction of CPD and registration categories. Amongst registration categories we are talking about simplifying, and it's likely that we will introduce a reduction of interpreter categories, so that we lose one. Equally, we are introducing categories, for example, translation and sign language to sign language (BSL to ISL for example). So, there is the beginning of a currency with NRCPD that is actively looking at what categories make sense, so I suppose if the field came to NRCPD and said 'We think this is worth looking at', the NRCPD would look at it. I don't have a strong view one way or another. I don't mean this to sound callous, but I don't have a strong view that they certainly shouldn't do it. But I do want them to be clear why they are doing it.

We asked if in Jim's view the impetus, or request for registration should come from ACSW or NATED for example.

I think it should come from the members - yes. It should come from the constituent body. Either employers and/or the workforce to say, actually, we think this would really work. With the NRCPD there is interest around public protection. And I can see, legitimately, that if appropriately qualified and registered CSWs were working in education, then there is an element of public protection that is appropriate. I don't have a problem with that. So, that's the principal bit. Then you get to the detail.

Barriers to Registration?

We pressed Jim to comment on whether, in view of his comments, a CSW category would therefore be achievable, or if there were other hidden barriers.

I think it should be something to consider. At least with all registration categories, one of the things that we are trying to do well is strip it back to the same principals, which are 1) What does the industry say are the National Occupational Standards (NOS) for a role? 2) Define a qualification for the role, 3) Work out whether we can proceed to a registration category. So, what we've done with the Level 6 in translation is, we went back to the field, we got them to define the occupational standards for translating from written English to BSL, or vice versa, and we've now got to the point where the qualification is developed and we have the NOS. We've said to NRCPD

'It's your choice, but you may want to consider this as a registration category.' So, the pattern is there.

We asked, would the same apply to a category for CSWs? We have the qualification, we have the NOS, we have the demand from the workforce, so hopefully we can proceed to registration.

Jim: Yes, that's right.

That was deemed a good point to sum up on. We commented that 2012 is the silver jubilee of the qualified CSW, and that it would be a tying together of loose ends if we can include in the CSW book that we finally have registration.

Jim: Well, get them to write to NRCPD.

We commented that negotiations are already under way. Thanks were exchanged and the interview closed.

9

Recent Views:
Head of Sensory Service

Interview: Wednesday 8 February 2012

This report is written anonymously, so is presented in the first person because it results in smoother grammar. Anonymity allows the writer to express views more freely and delivers the report from requiring lengthy checks and potential unwelcome amendments. The report is as follows:

In 2002, the Sensory Service I lead in the local authority first employed **communication support workers** (CSWs) to work with a young person who had made a decision to leave a school for the Deaf to go into mainstream education, so that person needed full British Sign Language (BSL) support. However, I was familiar with the CSW role before because one of the Local Authority provisions, a secondary school, was already employing CSWs. The model there was to have Teachers of the Deaf, CSWs and Deaf Instructors as a team.

That is partly where the local authority model came from. As a Teacher of the Deaf I had been conversant with the idea of support workers working alongside profoundly Deaf young people in classroom settings from when I trained, but they weren't called CSWs then. The first time I came across CSWs was when I was working for a school for the Deaf because there was a CSW course at the local Further Education (FE) College. I was in the area from 1995 to 2001 and was aware of people in the late nineties training on that course. In the school for the Deaf, some staff were similar in status to CSWs, but were at that time called tutors. They had the ability to work independently but under the supervision of the teachers, similar to the role of unqualified teachers.

CSWs – Different Status to Support Assistants

The model I use now in the local authority places CSWs on the unqualified teacher's pay scale which means they have a different status to support assistants. In the nineties, staff with similar roles were called tutors, but now, perhaps we might call them CSWs. I am aware that the acronym CSW is given to a whole range of roles that people fill with different pay scales, different conditions of service etc. The model in the Sensory Service I lead is more defined and a very distinct role which carries with it an expectation of having a certain level of qualification. CSWs are therefore employed on the unqualified teacher's pay scale, which carries exactly the same conditions as a teacher. The reason for this is that the local authority wanted to give the CSW role a particular status in order to attract people of a particular calibre into the role. That comes with certain levels of expectation as to how they will discharge their responsibilities. Within my local authority, the role of CSW is a very professional, significant career opportunity, and because

CSWs are employed as unqualified teachers, there is an expectation that they will undertake independent teaching. They will take on board teaching tasks that teachers are expected to do. The role of the CSW is seen not just as someone who interprets or communicates or provides sign or notes to give access to the spoken information in the classroom: within the local authority setting the CSWs are educators. They are involved in the education of the young people they support. They have an expectation of doing tutorial work, preparing and adapting materials. Some CSWs have a particular responsibility for audiology or for other aspects of provision to Deaf young people. All CSW activities may be similar to what a Teacher of the Deaf might do, but these things have to be done under the supervision of a Teacher of the Deaf. That is quite distinct from what some people would understand a CSW to be. To illustrate this, allow me to explain what happened during a recent recruitment drive for CSWs. One referee – who is also in Deaf education - responded in writing to criticise the job description the local authority have for a CSW for including such items as 'monitoring of amplification equipment' without understanding that this is what the local authority has created a CSW role to be.

CSWs as Educators?

I pondered whether CSWs should be described as educators or perhaps actually, they are teachers, albeit on the unqualified teacher's pay scale. I am aware that the status quo is to demarcate job roles into separate disciplines, for example interpreter, speech to text reporter, lip-speaker and notetaker, each having their own qualifications, which means that the discrete job role for CSWs should be linked to the CSW qualification. That is how the local authority has viewed the role, but a much broader stroke is used than in some services. In my local authority the CSW qualification is the baseline, which means that all people who join the service as CSWs but don't actually have the qualification are immediately sent on the training course. The qualification contains elements about understanding Deafness, causes of Deafness, aspects of Deaf education and how to make education accessible to Deaf young people. That covers similar ground to what Teachers of the Deaf cover in their courses but obviously theirs is at masters degree level with a whole greater depth of intensity and understanding.

Is there a Trend in Support Strategy?

It is interesting to consider whether the support strategy required for the Deaf children and young people in my local authority has changed over recent years. I would say that generally it is variable, without an identifiable trend. However, when I started teaching, the profession was emerging from a very significant auditory/oral phase, so most young people who were profoundly Deaf were educated in an oral manner, unless they went to a school for the Deaf. If they were in a specialist provision (unit) the majority of the students were oral and it was only in schools for the Deaf that an alternative method of communication was seen, and that wasn't always consistent. Some schools used Paget-Gorman, sign supported English (SSE), BSL, Cued speech and other communication methods, for example. However, now it's different because it's recognised that the use of Sign Language within the education setting is extremely beneficial for many profoundly Deaf people. Not necessarily all of them might want to use BSL or need it, but they do benefit from its use because it can be used to support the acquisition of English in the very early years. As to the change in the Deaf children and young people themselves, one important change is increasing cochlear implantation. The change is perhaps slower in my local authority than in other authorities, but the shift is significant.

Cochlear Implantation (CI)

Historically, parents with newly diagnosed Deaf babies and older Deaf children have been very comfortable with the model presented to them by Teachers of the Deaf in my local authority: i.e. to describe the full range of communication options for their children and to offer high quality support in the methodology chosen. Parents were often very happy to embrace signing and the whole ethos of Deaf Culture. There were proportionately few children, compared to some other areas, who were CI users and parents were often happy for them to be in a provision where the model of communication is Total Communication (that is SSE, BSL, whatever is successful in supporting language development including spoken language). Increasingly more parents of newly diagnosed, profoundly Deaf babies now want their children to have cochlear implants and this has an impact on the methodology that is used with the children, with parents now often choosing an auditory oral school provision. Although the children will have learnt to communicate via sign language as newborns, without there being any deliberate choice to change, the children naturally start to gravitate away from a full signing method of communication and some become completely oral. There is however, a varied range of communication requirements within my local authority cohort of Deaf children and young people, so naturally, some require fluent BSL support. This means that the local authority team contains some qualified interpreters. However, their role within the team remains that of a CSW. For example, when recruitment is carried out specifically for CSWs who have a very high level of signing, suitable for working in a higher education setting, the local authority recruits them as CSWs because they need to accommodate and embrace that broader CSW role. I believe that the people who work effectively, even in a higher education setting, are those who understand the educational aspect of the role in addition to the transmission of information that a conventional interpreter would aim to do. Within my team there is a collective ambition that CSWs will achieve at least BSL level 3 (not quite there yet) and that is a continuing goal. If a staff member has an interpreter qualification then that is a clear distinction of that person's ability. That doesn't necessarily mean that people with level 3 are not extremely skilled.

Communication Needs of the Individual

The important point is that staff have the ability to meet the communication needs of the individual they are working with – that may not depend on their level of signing qualification. Because of that I find that people without interpreter qualifications, who have or are working towards BSL Level 3, can still communicate extremely effectively with a range of Deaf students. Having said that, I recognise that it wouldn't be appropriate to put such staff into a higher education setting, where students are doing academic degrees. What enables staff to communicate effectively at BSL Level 3 or even below, is an understanding of Deafness and development, which is gleaned from having the CSW qualification. The CSW course teaches the implications of Deafness in terms of cognition, or how thinking and language develops in Deaf people; it teaches the impact on social and emotional development; what the challenge must then be for those Deaf young people in accessing mainstream education for themselves; it imparts a perception of what needs to be adapted, changed, modified. There needs to be a broad range of understanding about Deafness – not just about how well an individual can communicate something in sign. So, for example, in the local authority service some staff are extremely skilled with some students that are on vocational courses. Those students are not high ability students and staff need to be (and are) very skilled and naturally intuitive, as well as building up their knowledge and skills through training, about what is required to support them most effectively. That is at one end of the spectrum, then at the other end, some staff may be given short notice assignments, when we say "Right, John is doing a psychology lecture over at the University, can you do it?" and they can respond positively despite the linguistic demands being very challenging.

CSW Role Misunderstood by Many

I understand that a lot of people find it difficult to understand the role of a CSW, especially people travelling the interpreting route who say, "CSWs are just lower class interpreters, or less skilled interpreters", whereas the role of the CSW is not bound by interpreting, but rather (broadly) it is to provide access for Deaf young people to the curriculum, or the education that they are securing for themselves. My local authority have CSWs working at the compulsory school age, but some students choose to stay in education after that compulsory stage – that is what they have chosen for themselves – and the CSWs role is to provide access. That's the broad role, but there are so many different strands to providing access. I encourage CSWs to take all these things seriously, and carefully prioritise which training is appropriate to match each of the students they are working with. It depends on the communication requirements of those students. Some might be able to express what their communication needs are, but some may not always know, so staff need to know something about their degree of deafness; about the history of the development of their language skills; if they are cochlear implant users; if they have had these a long, or short time; what is their history, or family background, and what impact that has had; what audiological support have they had or continue to choose to use (because some students choose not to use amplification aids) so staff need to know why that is important and what difference it has made to the students' lives in terms of 'hearing' information about them, i.e: understanding spoken language and using spoken language.

CSWs Working as a Team

Staff need to understand how to support and develop language in students, not just spoken language but also sign language. Some students present at 16+ who have very weak signing skills themselves (although they are signers and it's their first language) so staff need to understand that. CSWs need to work alongside the ToD, the Speech and Language Therapist (SALT) to look at the linguistic aspects of what they are doing. They need to do the same with spoken language also. Students arrive with their own internalised language, so if staff are going to provide a careful, rigorous match of provision to what their abilities are, they need to know what that internalised language level is, and what the next developmental step is. For example an assessment may be carried out on a student of chronological age 16 plus - some may be found to be operating linguistically on a 7 or 8 year old level, so staff need to think, 'OK how am I going to move this student along?'. But at the same time they have to access a curriculum that is geared toward 16 year olds with a linguistic level of average 16 year olds. Staff need to understand how to bring those two mis-matches together. The team also needs to understand cognitive development because some of the students arrive with cognitive structures which are quite delayed and immature. They may seem to be very child-like and impulsive and some mainstream teaching staff are perturbed because they do not behave like 16 year olds. But the sensory team understands that is their developmental level because of all these background factors in their lives. Staff therefore need to take those students from where they currently are and move them onto the next appropriate emotional and cognitive phase. I see my team of CSWs being directly involved in that process. It's tough, so it should be always done with the supervision and support of people who hold the ToD qualification, and the SALT with a specialism in deafness, and a Deaf instructor, who has a profound understanding of how BSL is a living language for a Deaf person. It is also important to liaise with Educational Psychologists and therapists from Child and Adolescent Mental Health Service (CAMHS). The local authority has a CAMHS manager who visits and supports the Service to understand the psychology of young people, so they can use and adapt that for the teenagers who are Deaf and understand what impact psychology has on their development. All those things are put into the package, and the understanding of what needs to be known in order to meet the student's needs. If CSWs work within such a team it works very effectively because goals can be set and there is shared understanding and knowledge.

Using Freelance Interpreters

In my view, freelance interpreters may struggle to be able to work in school settings if they have not had training in education, deafness and development. I am not aware if that model has been created anywhere, although someone might buy-in a freelance interpreter if they need emergency cover for staff who are absent. If people want to work in a variety of places out in the community, that can only be done as a freelance interpreter. However, if an interpreter for his or her own professional development is willing to work with a group of Deaf young people and with a team of staff with a range of skills, share those skills and work as a member of the team, this could be a very positive thing to do. It might then be a springboard to working as a freelance interpreter because that person can then go into different settings and be confident about his or her versatility. This view should not be misconstrued as overconfidence, but I firmly believe that my local authority understanding of the CSW role is what others should aspire to. Within the team there is tremendous collaboration, because no one person has a complete set of skills. When different staff support the same student at different times, they work together to share signs, to create subject-specific signing/communication and other educational resources to make the best provision they can for that student.

Overriding Aim – Best Outcome for the Students

The perception is that what CSWs do well is not for themselves, but what provides the best outcomes for the student. I see the genuine excitement from CSWs when their student is making progress. When asked, they can describe the different aspects of support that have been brought together to make that progress occur – obviously they are a pivotal part of that success – together with ToDs, SALTs, Deaf Instructors. It is important also to work effectively with class teachers who are there to be amenable, flexible and work collaboratively. That engenders an aspiration to excellence. Seeing what other people do and achieve generates an aspiration in the team as a whole – that works well when the bar is set high enough.

Some of my local authority CSWs have achieved teaching qualifications, from 16 plus teaching qualifications up to post-graduate level within the context of the team because they recognise that having those teaching skills immeasurably adds to their role. Some develop niche skills – some CSWs are very interested in audiology and have taken that to quite an extensive level and understand much of what ToDs are required to know. Some CSWs in the team have taken on the challenge of assessment arrangements for students. I know personally that this is a really complex field because I used to be an examinations officer myself, and I know that it is considerably more complex than it was. Some are becoming experts in many different parts of media and ICT (Information and Communications Technology), and that creates an ethos of excellence and high aspiration that helps to promote and develop the students' progress.

I would like to see this model of the CSW role promoted more widely. I see it as a discrete role that profoundly benefits the Deaf children and young people the CSW works with. It is a robust model that challenges a view of CSWs as being merely 'less skilled interpreters', or that CSWs have too many roles to perform. I have also observed that this model promotes staff retention, almost as a side-effect, and that even when aspiring interpreters pass through, they are able to construct an explicit understanding of Deaf educational development, cognition and language, and leave with a strong understanding of collaboration and a desire to constantly improve skills. All of this conspires to stand them in good stead for a future career as an interpreter.

10
The Struggle for Recognition

Harrington (2001) states that the title 'Communication Support Worker' (CSW) is a role that is unique to the UK. Why this should be the case is unclear. It appears that other countries have not developed a CSW role for their workforce, but use sign language interpreters to provide communication support within the educational domain. It is not possible to state conclusively whether the UK was right or not to develop the role of the CSW. This is a question that is open to much discussion. Clearly, during the 1980s, the sudden increasing demand to provide appropriately trained personnel to offer communication support to Deaf students in further education and training needed addressing urgently. The funding offered by the Manpower Services Commission (MSC) coincided with the introduction of training schemes for young unemployed people. This funding enabled schemes to be developed to train people to provide communication support and greater access to young Deaf people wanting to enter further education. Hence the first communicator training scheme commenced in Birmingham in 1986.

Criticisms

Almost as soon as training for CSWs was formalised in the late 1980s, the criticisms began and, it appears, have never really ceased. Constructive criticisms can be extremely useful, when based on accurate facts. However, criticisms towards CSW training have often appeared to be made without consideration of the big picture and usually from people with little or no understanding of the role and its origins.

Formal training for communicators, later to be known as CSWs, started in the late 1980s, thanks initially to funding made available by the MSC. The training was robust, entry criteria were set and, regardless of criticisms received at the time about the training and the calibre of candidates, the number of qualified CSWs increased and entered the workforce. The ever growing numbers of young Deaf people wanting to take part in further education and, in particular YTS (Youth Training Schemes) were slowly able to do so, with appropriate communication support. However, concerns were soon raised by Warren Nickerson and Chris Green, trainers on the original courses in Birmingham and Derby, about the spread of subsequent communicator training schemes and courses across the country. It appears that certain underlying principles that were deemed essential in the full time national pilot schemes were not being enforced by MSC when funding further schemes. However, despite the growing criticisms, Nickerson and Green (1992) commented:

'Those people who believe that the money used by MSC

for communicator training schemes should have been used to fund 'interpreter' training, have failed to grasp the reality of post 16 education and the logic behind the funding. The final judgement on the value of communicator training will be in the hands of Deaf people themselves. The question to be answered is "Have opportunities for the education and training for Deaf people been enhanced because of the rise of the communicators?" (Green and Nickerson, 1992, pvi).

Concerns

Concerns continued to be raised throughout the 1990s and early 2000s. Rodgers (2000) talked about the concern that there still seemed to be insufficient numbers of CSWs to meet the ever-increasing demands of Deaf learners. Mention was made of some areas of the country where unqualified and inexperienced people attempted to provide communication support for Deaf learners. Clearly, reports such as this are indeed cause for concern. The question must be asked 'why are unqualified and inexperienced CSWs working in certain areas of the country?' Is this simply a matter of a lack of suitable training opportunities, or the fact that employers are unaware of the need for an appropriately trained CSW workforce? Rather than continue to criticise such examples of poor practice, surely it would be far better to try to address the problem and take positive steps to eradicate the situation.

In 2006, Karen Turner, Coordinator of CSWs and BFSWs (Bilingual Family Support Workers) at the Deaf and Hearing Impaired Team (DAHIT) in Leeds claimed that, in recent years, she had experienced difficulties in recruiting suitably qualified CSWs. This was deemed to be, at least partly, due to the demise of the Edexcel qualification for CSWs. The minimum requirements for employment as a CSW with DAHIT were stated to be:

BSL Stage 2 or equivalent functioning

GCSE English and Maths at Grade C or above

Edexcel qualification in Communication Support (preferably)

The report states 'it is proving very difficult at the moment to find people who have those skills' (Turner, 2006). Faced with such dilemmas, what are employers expected to do? Do they reject applications from Deaf students as they are unable to recruit appropriately qualified staff, or do they employ staff with lower than the minimum requirements and offer to train the staff once they are in post? It is reasonable to assume that this situation has been replicated throughout the UK over a number of years. If this is indeed true, the situation where there are a great number of unqualified CSWs working in education is more easily understood.

If the number of unqualified CSWs in the workforce were the reason for such criticisms directed towards those in the role, then the negative attitudes could, perhaps, be justified and the problem could start to be resolved. However, criticisms appeared to start almost as soon as the role of the CSW was developed. Therefore, it appears that the root of the negative attitudes goes much deeper than this.

CSWs Engaged in Interpreting

In 2002, a report, commissioned by the Department of Works and Pensions, was published, which, amongst other issues, raised concerns about the quality of CSWs in education:

'Communication Support Workers are usually engaged in educational settings to provide a range of services to Deaf students. Their responsibilities include interpreting, as well as note-taking and one-to-one tutorials with Deaf students.

Considerable criticism was expressed by Deaf people at the public meetings of people with Stage 1 and Stage 2 BSL qualifications being employed in these posts and, in addition, that they were being expected to interpret within the college in which they were employed. In the view of the Deaf people who raised this issue, these qualifications do not equip Communication Support Workers to be able to communicate to the standard required to support Deaf students in educational settings. They argued that they were in no position to provide interpreting services in educational or any other settings....... Some Deaf people therefore suggested that there was need to clarify the role of Communication Support Workers and, in particular, their role in relation to interpreters.' (Brien et al, 2002)

Professionals working in the educational domain with Deaf learners would agree. It is recognised that those Deaf learners who have advanced BSL language require staff with appropriate BSL to facilitate their learning. However, facilitating learning may require more than interpreting.

CSW Versus Interpreter

The issue of CSW versus interpreter is deeply rooted, but can be summarised as the difference between facilitating learning and interpreting. Often, those who perform the role of CSW have the interpreter mindset, therefore find it difficult to understand the educational role of the CSW, and can become very critical, especially upon qualifying as interpreters. The system does not help, because it is possible to find work as a CSW on the basis of holding BSL level 2 alone, and many people who want to become interpreters jump at the opportunity to use their budding bilingual skills. Around late August and early September each year, employers are often faced with the prospect of needing to support a greater number of Deaf students than expected, so are tempted to make use of those who are not appropriately qualified. It becomes a lottery because such folk may go on to become very skilled and qualified CSWs, but others may retain the interpreter mindset and use the 'system' to obtain their goal. That many interpreters are critical of those who do this is indicative of the problem. The CSW role and the Interpreter role should be viewed as different roles. However, many are adamant that the roles are the same, meaning that both roles are to facilitate interpreting. This view may be perpetuating the debate. It may be useful to discuss the difference by considering some 'interpreter objections' of the CSW role, and responses, so two are included here.

Objection 1

CSWs use the helper model of interpreting rather than the professional model. Deaf students are therefore perplexed when leaving education because they don't know how to access the proper interpreting role.

Response

An interpreting paradigm identified for use with adults should not be assigned to the role of CSW within the educational domain.

Explanation: Teachers of the Deaf are aware that young Deaf children do not understand the concept of interpreting and find it a cognitive 'leap too far' to differentiate between the person uttering the source language and the person who is interpreting. Deaf children up to indeterminate ages typically view a CSW as delivering information directly, despite having been told who is really speaking - they engage the person doing the interpreting rather than the teacher.

During what Jean Piaget defined as the preoperational stage (usually from 2 to 7 years), children are searching for 'representation.' (McLeod, 2009). They are learning how to move from the concrete to the abstract, and develop more abstract thought at around age 8-12, and at that stage Deaf children commence the journey toward understanding the concept of interpreting. However, where a child is functioning below average in school, or has delayed language development, due to Deafness and/or other reasons, the appreciation of interpreting may be delayed also.

It is a continuum of transition that is different for each Deaf child, and part of the responsibility of the educational team is to manage and promote it, aiming for completion before the transition from statutory education to further education (FE)/ higher education (HE). However where there are additional learning concerns or issues in cognitive development this may be delayed and continue well after leaving school. Interpreter training does not usually cover this concept. However, CSWs, as part of the educational team, share the responsibility to stimulate a proper understanding of the interpreting role, as part of an overall aim to promote independence. This is enshrined in the following extract from the application guide of the National Occupational Standards for Learning Support Staff who provide Communication Support (CSWs):

CP7.1CSW Know how to provide appropriate support that assists D/deaf learners' transition into and out of their current programme of learning.

This is done throughout the educational journey, but can be done in a very practical way, as part of the transitional aim when Deaf students are preparing to leave compulsory education. Each Deaf student leaves with a portfolio of useful contacts and advice about the 'big bad world' of interpreting.

CSWs co-research local services, together with the students, for example interpreting agencies, local Deaf services such as hearing aid centres, specific services for Deaf adults, advice on how to book an interpreter and obtain funding, how to apply for jobs and services that would require interpreting etc. We have seen this done with CSWs, who are at the frontline of this work, directed by the Teacher of the Deaf (ToD). This highlights the need for a concise educational team, with ToDs, teachers, CSWs, Deaf instructors and teaching assistants working as a team, with mutual aims. The team needs to have skills to do with assessing and enabling educational and language development that are not part of a general interpreting syllabus.

Objection 2

The role of CSW should be abolished, and interpreters only should be used to work with Deaf students in education, because Deaf people of all ages deserve the best in terms of language and interpreting.

Response

Deaf learners at all ages are truly representative of Deaf people in society, in terms of variations of levels of hearing, cognition and development. Most do not require an interpreter.

Explanation: Typically, interpreters work with profoundly Deaf BSL users. BSL training involves the search for BSL fluency. English must be dropped, Sign Supported English (SSE) must be dropped. The grammar of BSL, at first a mystery, slowly dawns, and a level of fluency is deemed appropriate enough for interpreter training to commence. That training involves learning how to interpret between English and BSL. When at last that goal has been achieved, that is what happens; an interpreter works between BSL and English. Those who require the services of such interpreters are BSL users. Sometimes a Deaf 'client' requests that an interpreter uses SSE, but interpreters often report that they find this difficult and a chore, because the whole emphasis of the learning journey has been on BSL. A qualified BSL/English interpreter therefore usually operates at the BSL extremity of the Deaf and hard of hearing range. This is borne out by the BSL Futures Project (2008) that had a budget of £2.7 million for training 30 individual interpreters in Wales. It was an ambitious project that was rightly hailed as a great success. However, the report on the project contained this comment from stakeholders:.

'Some stakeholders questioned the value for money of the project as it was likely to benefit only a relatively small number of people and a relatively small proportion of the overall spectrum of the Deaf and hard of hearing community.'

The report includes the following response:

"We are also aware of the argument that the investment has only benefited a narrow range of the Deaf community i.e. those who use BSL. Arguably, however, for those who are profoundly Deaf, this investment is essential if they are to have any chance of enjoying equality of access to public services and (potentially, at least) employment opportunities.' (BSL Futures Project, 2008).

By contrast, CSWs are required to operate much more widely, much further along the Deaf and hard of hearing range, toward the non-signing contingency, up to where the educational statements (therefore funding) appropriate for each Deaf learner do not apply. In 2011, the CRIDE Report (Consortium for Research into Deaf Education) stated that there are at least 34,927 Deaf children in England, but only 9% use sign language to some extent to communicate. Therefore, interpreters exclusively, should not be employed to work with Deaf students in education. Rather, appropriate staff should be used, including CSWs and interpreters, or perhaps better, an intelligent use of CSWs with interpreting qualifications.

The Quest for Registration

There has been talk of a registration system for CSWs since the early 1990s. Green and Nickerson (1992) stated they believed that NATED should establish a register of Communication Support Workers. The intention was to submit a motion to this effect to the NATED Annual General Meeting on 9 May 1992. The proposal was that:

'...this Register would be to ensure that all workers in the Post 16 sector have or are undergoing appropriate training. In the process of establishing such a Register, NATED would need to clearly identify benchmarks of competence and specify routes to training. Such a development is long overdue...' (Green and Nickerson, 1992, p214).

The register never materialised so it can only be presumed that either the motion was not passed, or that it was not submitted. Who can tell whether the development of such a register at this time would have helped to sway the constant waves of criticism against CSWs. We will never know. A few years later Simpson (2007) remarked:

'As for CACDP (Council for the Advancement of Communication with Deaf People) and its desire to establish a register of qualified Communication Support Workers, the ever increasing demands of National Vocational Qualifications (NVQs) and the external demands to establish a national framework of qualifications required an increasing amount of staff time. This, together with the burgeoning demand for sign language interpreters, working outside of further and higher education, undermined attempts to establish a register of qualified Communication Support Workers. It is a matter of regret that, by the end of the twentieth century, there was not a fully effective register able to give high quality support to a new generation of talented and ambitious young Deaf people.' (Simpson, 2007, p181).

Once again, the intention was there to develop a register for qualified CSWs. Once again, for whatever reason, the register never materialised.

Stewart Simpson was the first Chief Executive of CACDP (Council for the Advancement of Communication with Deaf People - now renamed as Signature). In 2000 Miranda Pickersgill took over that role. Miranda was aware of CACDP's intention, at some point, to develop a system of registration for CSWs. However, during her interview for this book in November 2011 she expressed a different view. She recalled that, after all the trouble of setting up a register for interpreters, people then did not always want to be regulated. With registration comes a complaints procedure, a disciplinary procedure. Registration can be removed or suspended for a period of time if deemed appropriate. The issue with sign language interpreters is that most are self-employed, therefore people are right to question whether anyone has the right to deny them their source of income. There needed to be a complaints committee and this, along with everything else, costs money. Complaints need to be investigated. Miranda tried to imagine what would happen if a complaint was raised about a CSW's level of BSL. What would the outcome be? The investigation would have to take place within the college.

Miranda's reluctance to agree to the setting up of a registration system for CSWs continues. She feels that if there is a need for some sort of recognition and regulation, then if it's possible to come up with something, it shouldn't be like the other National Registers of Communication Professionals with Deaf and Deafblind people (NRCPD) registration categories. She really believes it can't be the same because of the educational setting and role. Having said that, Miranda hopes it is resolved. She acknowledges that the progress that has been made is super. Regardless of the register, those other things – the discussions of the role, the use of relevant qualifications, the development of professional support - are hugely important. They were always more important than whether or not there should be a register.

Regardless of the views expressed above, if CSWs were to achieve a registration category within the NRCPD then, hopefully, this would at least start to address some of the criticisms. Registration would ensure that CSWs could be nationally recognised as professionals. In order to gain entry to the register, CSWs would need to provide evidence of appropriate qualification (Edexcel, Signature or equivalent) and a minimum of Level 3 in British Sign Language (BSL). Registration would require members to undertake regular continuing professional development (CPD) and thereby strive to improve and build on their skills. Naturally, registration could not be compulsory, but at least this would be a clear indication to employers of the minimum acceptable standards for CSWs.

The Fight Back

CSWs have been viewed by many as the underdogs for a considerable number of years. CSWs are often thought to be interpreters-in-waiting, as though the ultimate goal for anyone involved in supporting communication with Deaf people should be that of an interpreter. Is it any wonder then, that CSWs are regarded as less worthy than interpreters. The role of the CSW needs to be made clear. CSWs are not, and have never been, any less able or worthy than interpreters. The main issue is that the roles of CSW and interpreters are distinctly different and should be recognised as such.

National Occupational Standards

'Close the Gap' was an NDCS (National Deaf Children's Society) campaign in 2008. The campaign focused on educational underachievement by Deaf children in England. NDCS recommendations from this campaign included a call for the Government to develop national standards for the delivery of specialist support.

Happily, thanks to funding made available through the I-Sign Project, National Occupational Standards (NOS) for CSWs were developed in 2010 and are now available for use by CSWs, employers and learning provider organisations.

A concise explanation of the application of NOS for CSWs is given here:

An Application of the National Occupational Standards for Learning Support Staff who provide Communication Support.

Adapted from the Application Guide produced by Signature in association with NATED, ACSW and LLUK, available online at: http://www.signature.org.uk/documents/Deaf_learners_guide.pdf

The application guide defines the skills, knowledge and understanding that any communication support worker will need to support Deaf learners.

It is an application of the National Occupational Standards for Learning Support Staff. These standards were approved in 2008 and describe, in generic terms, the skills, knowledge and attributes required of those who perform the wide variety of learning support roles under-taken with learners and employers. The standards are context free and level free.

An application guidance document such as this, provides more detail for the standards where this is considered of value. Application guidance documents can be written for any suite of standards.

They can be written for a particular context such as offender learning, for a particular subject such as literacy and numeracy or for a particular group of learners or users, as in this document for learning support practition-ers with a focus on Deaf learners.

Application guidance documents are produced through consultation with stakeholders and the relevant commu-nity of practice. This application guide has been produced by Signature in association with the National Association for Tertiary Education for Deaf People (NATED), The Association of Communication Support Workers (ACSW) and Lifelong Learning UK. This is in response to the Government-funded, I-Sign Project, whose overall aim is to improve the status and provision of British Sign Language (BSL) for Deaf children and families. One of the strands within the project was to develop a qualifica-tion for the workforce who support Deaf learners. This can raise the status and recognise the professionalism of the communication support workforce. Signature was the lead body in this development, and has been working closely with NATED and ACSW to achieve the outcome.

Communication support workers may use the guidance to:

- Identify professional development needs in relation to supporting Deaf learners
- Develop new skills
- Develop existing skills to meet the specific needs of Deaf

learners.

Learning provider organisations/employers may use the guidance to:

- Illustrate how the National Occupational Standards (NOS) for the role of learning support practitioner in the lifelong learning sector apply to the delivery of learning support to Deaf learners
- Develop and offer a framework for training and continuing professional development for learning support practitioners working with Deaf learners
- Identify and disseminate effective practice in the delivery of learning support for Deaf learners
- Support the development of learning support practitioner job descriptions
- Motivate and assist learning support practitioners to develop a range of specialist skills to support Deaf learners
- Map current provision and performance against the standards to improve the quality of learning support provision
- Inform appraisal objectives and peer reviews
- Ensure that all staff have the skills to make a full contribution to the success of their organisation in a demand led and changing environment.

Learning support practitioner educators and awarding organisations may use the guidance to:

- Develop new qualifications
- Develop guidance on qualifications
- Map current provision against the standards
- Support curriculum development, delivery and assessment.

The learning support role

Lifelong Learning UK continues to develop and refine

the description of the learning support role. The role of learning support practitioners was described during the development of the first National Occupational Standards for Learning Support Staff in 2007.

Learning support practitioners work under the direction of a person leading the learning. They contribute to the provision of learning opportunities that promote the achievement and progression of the learners they support. Important aspects of their role identified included:

- to provide learning support for individuals and/or groups
- to work with others to provide learning support
- to promote learner independence and self-determination
- to promote inclusion and participation.

As part of the research to develop NOS, Lifelong Learning UK identified two types of learning support role:

- A generalist role: the practitioner has knowledge, understanding and skills across a wide range of provision and contributes to the support of learners with a range of differing needs and/or over a range of settings.
- A specialist learning support role: the practitioner has expertise in learning support but also has knowledge, understanding and skills in a particular area or aspect of learning provision. The practitioner applies their expertise in learning support to this particular area or aspect of provision.

Most responsibilities are common to both roles, but are contextualised for the role with an area of specialism. Although the role is described as having an area of specialism, this does not mean that learning support practitioners should be referred to as specialists. The level of responsibility and training expected of this role clearly does not warrant the use of this term. At the time of consultation on the standards, and the piloting of the role, representatives of learning providers were concerned that these practitioners should not be considered as specialists in the area or aspect of learning provision. In particular, there should be as clear a distinction as possible between this role and that of teachers, in the same area of learning or aspect of provision. Although we draw attention to the element of specialism here, in practice this need not be reflected in job titles or other references to the role.

The context for communication support work

This application guide applies the generic NOS to the effective delivery of learning support to Deaf learners. As with any learner, those who are Deaf engage in a range of programmes in a variety of settings. The scope of this guide covers learning Support Practitioners supporting learners in:

- A discrete programme of learning, for example those in a specialist college who may be accessing independent, vocational or pre employment programmes
- A targeted programme of learning designed to meet the needs of a specific group of learners, for example a targeted mental health programme
- A mainstream programme of learning, for example a vocational or academic course such as a BTEC Diploma in Sports and Leisure alongside their non-disabled peers.

In addition, the standards recognise that practitioners may carry out a broad range of support roles. For example, those providing learning support for Deaf learners may also have communication responsibilities. Where a combination of support roles are performed, these should be underpinned by the standards taken from the appropriate specialism. A role combining learning support with communication responsibilities would therefore be underpinned by the NOS for Learning Support Practitioners and the standards for Communication Support Workers.

This application guide is targeted at a learning support role in an area of specialism and is designed for learning support practitioners with a focus on Deaf learners (communication support worker).

A Deaf learner may be found in any setting and studying at any level. Their needs are often around communication, access to learning and the adjustments that organisations, teachers and learning support practitioners make to ensure they can engage effectively in learning.

It is important to recognise that Deaf learners can be affected by the specific degree of Deafness or hearing loss, and the impact on learning can vary depending on the extent of the Deafness or hearing loss. A learning support practitioner will need to gather information from the Deaf learner, and the person(s) leading the learning, to identify the best strategies and resources for supporting the learning process.

Stronger Together

One very positive change in recent years has been the move towards a greater working relationship between NATED, ACSW and Signature. Whereas in the past there had been resistance and a reluctance to work together, a positive bi-product of the I-Sign Project was the development of a strong working relationship between the three organisations.

In 2010 Maria Bailey was invited to join the committee of NATED as a co-opted member. Since that date she has attended NATED committee meetings, presenting regular updates on Signature developments and seeking feedback where appropriate. Andy Owen became a co-opted committee member of

NATED in 2009 as a representative of ACSW. As a result of these changes, a greater understanding and mutual respect has formed between all stakeholders. This collaboration continues to aid identification of concerns and the development of training for CSWs which will, hopefully, enable them to be recognised as the true professionals that they are.

As always, there will be some who do not agree with these sentiments. The aim now is to attempt to disprove all of the misconceptions and continue to strive for CSW recognition and acceptance. There is still a mountain to climb, but at least we have started the ascent.

11
ACSW Development Timeline

In March 2005, a Yahoo group was set up by a **communication support worker** (CSW) named Mary Black, who was concerned about the lack of support for CSWs. She set up the group with the aim of providing a forum for CSWs to discuss their concerns. Soon Liana Lloyd, also working as a CSW, joined the group which very quickly proved to be popular. A flurry of postings showed that their concerns were felt by others also.

Tuesday 13th June 2006. ASLI Meeting

The Association of Sign Language Interpreters (ASLI) held an open meeting on the subject of CSWs. The meeting, attended by Mary and Liana, took place at the Friend's Meeting House in the Euston Road, London and had two parts. The first larger debate issued around CSWs and the second was about ASLI and their business, in particular, how to raise funds for ASLI.

The meeting commenced with a general debate about CSWs. Some expressed the view that CSWs needed the same as the members of ASLI, in terms of support and training. Some people felt that the role of the CSW needed to be more clearly defined, so that people knew what was expected of them, and also they needed a clearer view of their boundaries. There was discussion about whether the role varied depending on the different needs of particular educational locations, such as schools, colleges, etc.

It was noted that CSWs had their own Yahoo group, and that after the meeting with ASLI, they could use that informal group as a springboard into something more concrete. There was some discussion about an appropriate formal qualification for CSWs and that perhaps CSWs could somehow be attached to ASLI so that the knowledge, expertise and experience of ASLI's members could be shared. In return, some kind of remittance could be given to ASLI.

ASLI representatives advised CSWs to use all their contacts to compile some action points for the upcoming months, to plan meetings, decide agendas, discuss training needs etc. and inform ASLI, bearing in mind always a link with income generation. ASLI suggested that at their next meeting, scheduled to take place on 10th Oct 2006, an update could be presented on any progress made and a report tabled detailing what CSWs would like to see from ASLI. At that point, the meeting turned its discussion to the second item on the agenda, which was how more revenue could be generated for ASLI.

After the ASLI Meeting

No formal minutes of the meeting on 13th June 2006 have been made available, but several people made detailed notes. Some felt that ASLI were disinterested and were treating CSWs as an income-generating opportunity. Others felt that the focus on the British Sign Language (BSL) skills of CSWs, being less than those of interpreters, engendered an air of superiority, but that at least some individuals in ASLI were holding out an olive branch of sorts. It was difficult to identify whether there was an overt 'official' ASLI stance or not. Some felt that ASLI representatives had made their apologies and were not willing to formally offer CSWs any concrete offer of affiliation, certainly not without a membership referendum. In any case, it was left to no one except a motley group of individual CSWs to make some sort of response or decision. Some felt elated in the knowledge that they could rely on no one except themselves to make something of the void, but there was still that void to overcome. The only entity was a humble Yahoo group.

Monday 18th Sept 2006, Starbucks Oxford Street

Following the ASLI meeting, the Yahoo group received several requests for the setting-up of a formal CSW association. On Wednesday 21st June, Andy Owen emailed Mary Black and Liana Lloyd, the group moderators, and suggested a face to face meeting to discuss that very issue. It was delayed, however, because the long educational summer holiday was required to recharge CSW batteries.

A meeting was eventually arranged for Monday 18th September in the basement of Starbucks in Oxford Street, on the corner of Soho Square where the Football Association has its headquarters. Andy arrived with a plan on how to set up an association, a draft constitution and research on structure. He had never met Mary or Liana but the trio seemed to spark off a mutual understanding. A plan of action was devised over cappuccinos, and before the three felt they had overstayed their welcome and the tables were being cleared, they agreed on organising the first meeting of the Association of Communication Support Workers (ACSW), to take place as soon as viable the following month.

Monday 19th Oct 2006, Acton Deaf Centre

It was a cool dark autumn evening when a group of CSWs converged on a busy crossroads and entered the converted shop on the corner which was the Acton Deaf Centre. At the agreed start time about fifteen people had arrived so Mary commenced the meeting. She introduced herself as a working CSW/PA (Personal Assistant) since 2003, and Liana Lloyd and Andy Owen introduced themselves. Two other CSWs took part: Lauren Loughnane took notes and Vicky Nunn volunteered to interpret, although this was not required.

Those present were asked to get into three groups led by Mary, Liana and Andy to discuss what they would like the association to consider, then each group fed back. Here is the feedback in full:

Group 1

Mission statement. Lobby for greater understanding of what we do, recognition of role. Better awareness of our professional role. Support with ethical dilemmas. Professional Body – insurance/union. Lobby for or provide cheaper courses/training.

Group 2

Standardisation of the role including pay. Training. Code of Ethics. Support (job rights/legal advice). Insurance.

Group 3

CSW register, official standards. Information, classification. Power to lobby organisations. Training. CSW register. Flexibility – inclusion of Notetakers.

Other suggestions: Information for employers on CSW's. Pay scale. Appropriate dress. Freelance support. Key worker loan. Minimum wage. Newsletter. Recognise difference between CSWs and interpreters. Social. Mission statement.

The three groups merged again and there followed a general discussion. Mary reported that ASLI were interested to learn about what would transpire from the meeting because they would like to work with ACSW. Indeed, the Chair of ASLI had asked for a report as soon as possible in order to commence negotiations.

There were comments about the assistance of ASLI being valuable, but the preference was for a separate group for CSWs. Mary compared the relative numbers: around 300 Interpreters in the UK and about 4,000 CSWs. Therefore membership potential was massive and ACSW could become a very strong association and wield a voice for change. However, Mary brought the meeting to order and the need to focus on getting set up. The aim was to get all CSWs involved but obviously the initial need was for some CSWs to be entrusted to make decisions.

CSW Register

Mary spoke about creating an online register for CSWs. She spoke of the importance of the association not to be solely London based and called for volunteers. There was discussion about the register being subdivided possibly into BSL levels and CSW qualification.

One CSW who attended the ASLI meeting commented that CSWs do not have the same role as interpreters, so there would be a problem fitting into ASLI. Indeed, the feeling was that ASLI's stance was somewhat condescending, and that their constant mistaken emphasis on the BSL levels of CSWs betrayed a misunderstanding of the CSW function. Mary agreed that CSWs have a different role to interpreters, but that ACSW should at least have links with ASLI.

Andy spoke in general about Professional Indemnity Insurance (PII). He explained the ASLI method — that members are automatically covered by PII, but that he had his own private insurance, not from ASLI. Andy spoke of three different types of insurance: Trade Indemnity Insurance, Public Liability Insurance and PII, which provides cover if the client sues, for example if they feel they failed in some way because communication was not adequate, or if the client feels that confidentiality was breached. Andy explained that CSWs needed a much more flexible cover, tailored to individual CSWs' needs, and not limited to membership of ACSW.

Mary explained that when ACSW had enough members a tender could go out for appropriate PII for CSWs, but that the issues needed to wait until the association was set up and then more lengthy discussions could take place on these and other topics, such as training and qualifications.

By the time the meeting closed at 9pm, interim measures were agreed: Interim Chair (Mary), Interim Secretary (Andy) and Interim Administrator (Liana), and Vicky Nunn volunteered for an interim period as Treasurer. The call for a volunteer for the role of Interim Membership Secretary was met with silence, so the role remained open. All was agreed on a general 'Aye'.

Saturday 10th Feb 2007, See Hear

The BBC screened a 'See Hear' interview with Mary Black on Saturday 10th February 2007, repeated on Wednesday 14th. Mary explained the rationale of the new association, and announced a meeting the very next month. Congratulations were received for the favourable screening and it was generally felt that this contributed to the success of the AGM, which took place shortly after the See Hear programme.

March 2007, ACSW Annual General Meeting

The AGM took place at the historic St Anne's church, Dean Street London, on a warm March day. An entrance fee was charged to cover the venue and refreshment costs, but the worries that enough people would turn up to cover costs were unfounded. The interim committee members had paid for various things from their own pockets up until then, so were hoping for some financial support. As it happened, the meeting was well attended by over fifty people – CSWs, Managers, Deaf people and other interested parties. The geographic spread was wide: people attended from all over the country, the furthest being Edinburgh. The meeting was supported by two trainee interpreters and an electronic notetaker, who all very kindly gave up their time voluntarily.

Judith Collins Keynote

The first speaker was Judith Collins, Teaching Fellow & BSL Coordinator, Durham University Language Centre, who gave a thought-provoking presentation about her view of CSWs from a Deaf perspective, and the future of CSWs. She expressed concern about the over-modification of students' work by CSWs, even suggesting that some students had achieved qualifications without the appropriate independent skills. She also suggested that CSWs should have a teaching qualification, and BSL NVQ level 4. These views generated many questions from the floor, from both Deaf and non-Deaf people. All were interested in what she had to say and many recognised that this may be something that needed discussion for the future.

After a short coffee break, the meeting moved onto the main

purpose of the day – the first ever Annual General Meeting for the Association of Communication Support Workers. Until this point, ACSW was not formally in existence, with only an interim committee since the first meeting back in October 2006. The association had been set up through all the formal legal channels, including registration with Companies House and Secretary of State approval. There was a logo, a website, a bank account, draft Constitution and meeting Standing Orders etc., but no company directors had been ratified. Also, up to and including the date of the AGM, there were no members of ACSW to decide anything by vote. It was a 'chicken and egg' problem. The first order of the meeting therefore was to propose an extra-ordinary motion that would allow the people present full voting rights for the purposes of that meeting only. This was essential so that certain proposals could be brought and decided. The motion was proposed and the vote was unanimous.

Interim Committee duly Ratified

Each member of the interim committee then presented a short PowerPoint presentation about their particular role in the association, explained what they had been doing to prepare for the ACSW current position, what they had achieved, and where they would like to go in the future. The interim committee had changed in the meantime, with Liana stepping down to concentrate on her interpreting studies (although she took a full part in aiding the meeting) and Paul Michaels stepping up to the mark for membership secretary. The following motions were then brought for the meeting to ratify:

1) Interim Committee
2) Regional representatives
3) Constitution and Standing orders

4) Membership policies and structure

5) E Group policy

6) Declaration of Professional Commitment

7) Logo policy

There was some healthy discussion during the course of this process, after which all the proposals were approved, some unanimously. The meeting was brought to a close with a plea for CSWs to let the Committee know their views, so that the duly ratified policies, structures and constitution etc. could begin the process of discussion and amendment.

Nicki Harris Keynote

The second keynote speaker then gave her presentation. This was Nicki Harris, Head of Post 16 Physical & Sensory Support Service, Surrey. After giving brief thanks for the first keynote speaker, Nicki spoke about the Sensory Team in Surrey (where CSWs are called SSWs – Student Support Workers). She spoke about the skills and qualities of a CSW, and about how their profile could be raised. She took the bull by the horns and dipped into the CSW versus interpreter debate, and spoke about funding. She rounded off with a call for networking with all interested groups, and a challenge for all CSWs to remember that the Deaf students deserve the best. Nicki's presentation was very well received with questions from the floor and a warm round of applause.

The afternoon was brought to a close with flowers and expressions of gratitude to all who were involved in the meeting. A prize mug (glazed with the proud words; 'I went to London') was presented to the person who had travelled the furthest … no surprises that it went to Emma Dunleavy from Edinburgh. Delegates then moved to a local more relaxing environment for informal networking.

The meeting was a resounding success, and the Association was officially up and running.

9th Feb 2008, ACSW Chelmsford Regional Meeting

Almost a year had passed before the next ACSW meeting took place on a sunny winter's Saturday in 2008. Despite the balmy weather, around sixty language service professionals chose to spend it inside the rooms of Chelmsford College, Moulsham Street.

There was an air of expectancy as the doors opened for registration. People drank tea and old friends hugged and caught up. The main room had windows along two sides, so the sunshine added to the atmosphere as the meeting started at about 10.45, earlier than published. Janice Daniels-Dey, regional ACSW representative who had arranged the meeting, commenced proceedings.

Jeanette Wright Keynote

The Keynote speaker, Jeanette Wright, was introduced. Jeanette explained, as the sun streamed through the windows, that in her opinion, Deaf clients should be able to exercise preference of human aids to communication; lipspeaker, interpreter, CSW etc. She said that simply booking an interpreter was not always the correct option due to levels of BSL being potentially too high. She explained that many Deaf students and adults do not have advanced BSL skills and may require alternative forms of communication. Jeanette called for information to be made available to Deaf people, such as information about the different communication support methods available to enable Deaf people to choose what they prefer, and be informed on how to use the personnel. Jeannette suggested that Access to Work may be an appropriate forum for disseminating such information, and a directory of CSWs should be available so that Deaf people can make their own choice. Jeanette was happy with a minimum of level 3 BSL for CSWs together with Deaf awareness qualifications.

The Chair then gave a presentation on the structure of the Association and the vacant roles that required volunteers to fill. She informed delegates about the new NATED (National Association for Tertiary Education for the Deaf) CSW Code of Practice, and said that it had the full support of ACSW. Members were also informed about a recent proposal to change the ASLI membership criteria to incorporate CSWs, and delegates were asked to discuss this on the ACSW forum. An interesting twist was that during the meeting, Mary Black took a private call from a prominent member of ASLI who explained that he was against CSWs being subsumed into ASLI and that he supported CSWs having their own association. What prompted the call was not clear.

The meeting was deemed a great success and produced twelve new members. ACSW Committee attendees: Chair (Mary Black) Secretary (Andy Owen) Treasurer (Vicky Nunn) Membership Secretary (Paul Michaels). Workshop Leaders were Kenneth Culver, Jill Bussien, Andy Owen and Vicky Nunn. Interpreters were Tracy Tyler, Tina Holmes and Vicky Mason, with Lipspeaker Linda Croton.

19th April 2008, AGM Leicester

At the very start of ACSW, there was a determination not to have a southern-only association, so in April 2008 the committee travelled up the M1 to Action Deafness, Welford Road, Leicester. It was match day for Leicester Tigers, who faced Bristol at the Welford Road stadium just around the corner. The keynote speaker was Jill Jones of the Deaf Ex-Mainstreamers group, continuing a burgeoning tradition of a Deaf keynote speaker. Jill spoke about, "Best Value Review and finding evidence base". She also presented a workshop on Continuous Professional Development (CPD). The discussions from that workshop dovetailed in nicely with the group work from the earlier meeting in Acton, and provided fuel for the CPD work that Jill Newlands was to pick up and champion in Derby the following year. At the meeting, members were asked to vote on a resolution to set up a register of qualified CSWs, following on from Jeanette Wright's impassioned appeal in Chelmsford. The resolution was duly passed, but a register of CSWs was destined to become an aspiration more than an immediate reality. At the AGM part of the meeting Mary Black stood down because she was due to emigrate, and Andy Owen became Chair. Paul Michaels resigned and Sabine Hagemes took over as Membership Secretary (unfortunately, later that year Sabine broke her leg, which meant that her work on the ACSW membership was curtailed).

As delegates left the venue, they mingled with elated Tiger supporters, whose team had beaten Bristol 32-14.

25th Sept 2008, 'Future of Registration' Meeting

On the 1st September 2008, the ACSW Chair received an email from CACDP's (Council for the Advancement of Communication with Deaf People) Paul Parsons. He explained that earlier that year CACDP had commissioned a report on the future of registration, and the next stage of the process required the input of professional organisations. Paul explained that ACSW and the Deaf Interpreter's Network (DIN) were invited because of the discussions about registering CSWs and Deaf professionals and offering registration categories for these professionals in the future. The 'Future of Registration' meeting was duly held from 6pm-8pm on 25 September 2008 at LVSRC (London Voluntary Sector Resource Centre), Holloway Road, London. Associations in attendance were: Association of Sign Language Interpreters; Association of Lipspeakers; Association of Verbatim Speech to Text Reporters; Association of Notetaking Professionals; Association of Communication Support Workers; ASLI Deaf Interpreters' Network. There was broad agreement about the inclusion of DIN and ACSW into a soon-to-be reconstituted register of professionals, and a general discussion followed about a possible name and its resulting acronym.

ACSW and ASLI Meeting 21st March 2009

This meeting took place at No. 68 Dean Street, a few doors along the street from where the AGM had taken place in March 2007. The house at No. 68, one of the great surviving examples of early Georgian architecture in London, was the setting where the ACSW committee met representatives from the ASLI Educational Working Group and Access To Work Working Group. It was an initial meeting to discuss mutual boundaries and possible collaboration.

Prior to the meeting, the ACSW committee met for a briefing in the basement at Starbucks, where Andy had met Mary and Liana for the first time in September 2006. They agreed a mutual goal of downplaying any perceived obstacles with the aim of a positive outcome. This was to be the first official meeting between the two associations and the ACSW aim was to be cordial and hospitable.

The meeting duly commenced, and after initial introductions, the agenda was discussed for some time with an increasing accusative – defensive tendency. Then followed some concise advice from one ASLI representative that ACSW should be closed down and support for CSWs should be discontinued because of recent news that the role was dying out. A new initiative to train many new interpreters was in the pipeline so there would be plenty to work in education and CSWs would not be required. She commented that if CSWs achieved registration she would eat her hat. However, there was a welcome for all to join ASLI.

Following these comments there was little appetite for verbal sparring. The ACSW committee had aimed for a positive outcome but it was clear it was not mutual. There was no discussion about 'date of next meeting' but merely a promise to circulate minutes for agreement. The minutes were duly prepared by ACSW's Lauren Loughnane and emailed to all who had attended, but upon return, any reference to the advice had been removed. The ACSW committee felt that the minutes should reflect a true account of the meeting so re-instated the references. The document remains undetermined.

It must be stated that, years later, one ASLI representative who was at that meeting expressed her regret and embarrassment at what had happened. It seemed that a potential meeting of minds was short-circuited. However, ACSW and ASLI were destined to sit around a different table in the not too distant future. Following the ill-fated meeting the ACSW committee had little time for introspection in the preparation for the 2009 AGM less than a month later. There was however, brief discussion over what hat to purchase in order to make a formal presentation after CSW registration had been achieved.

Derby AGM 18th April 2009

2009 saw the AGM again in the Midlands, hosted by Jill Newlands, ACSW Regional Representative, at the Rycote

Centre, Derby. The keynote speaker at this event was the irrepressible Peter Llewellyn-Jones who tackled the controversial subject, "Interpreter training for Level 2 CSWs". This broke the short tradition of a Deaf keynote speaker, but it was a timely encouragement to all CSWs attending, who appreciated Peter's erudite yet down-to-earth presentation. Peter also led a workshop on voice-over theory, which generated glowing feedback. The speech and language therapist Jane Thomas led an excellent workshop on 'Lexical Reinforcement', highly relevant because much of mainstream teaching and assessment is delivered in English. There were 'Hot Tips for better Notetaking' by Meriel Michaelides, who also kindly graced the meeting with electronic notes, and Jill Newlands picked up the baton of 'Continuous Professional Development'. It was at that meeting that members agreed a motion on setting up a postal voting instrument, giving absent members an opportunity of having a voice. Also, Matt Brown, who had been acting in the membership secretary role, was duly voted in.

Near to the close of the meeting, a report was given by Cathy Barnes of Signature about the future of CSW registration. It was a courteous report containing bones only. A question and answer session may have yielded some flesh but time was out. With the caretaker standing by, Andy Owen was constrained to offer thanks and close the meeting. Feedback was effusive and appreciative.

Attending an ACSW meeting for the first time was Maria Bailey, who had just been given the responsibility by Signature of heading the work on a proposed new CSW qualification. Maria's relationship with ACSW was destined to be closely interconnected. NATED also held their 2009 AGM in Derby, just 3 months later. Maria Bailey presented at that event and in questions and answers, CSWs had much to tell of their views. In the following year ACSW and NATED were to develop a strong working relationship, culminating in a thoroughly successful joint conference. This was partly due to the ACSW Chair being co-opted onto the NATED committee (attending his first meeting on the 30th April 2009) but perhaps more to the mutual understanding and outlook of the two associations.

NATED

In 2009, the National Association for Tertiary Education for Deaf People (NATED), a well-established organisation, with roots going back to 1976, was undergoing something of a re-launch. Early in 2007, NATED had developed the Code of Practice for CSWs after national consultations, and held the traditional Standards for CSWs. However, it appeared that NATED was overlooked and ACSW was contacted instead when Signature decided to develop a new qualification for CSWs. ACSW aided Signature in disseminating a questionnaire about the proposed CSW qualification, but an 'E' was added and it was dubbed the 'ECSW' qualification, as if somehow it needed underlining that the overwhelming majority of CSWs work in education. Unfortunately the questionnaire asked: 'In your opinion, are Educational Communication Support Workers part of a wider group of classroom support workers called Learning Support Practitioners, or is yours a different role?" It struck a raw nerve for those CSWs who were constantly explaining to subject tutors that they were not teaching assistants.

Maria Bailey was called into the stew. One of her first jobs was to smooth the ruffled feathers left by the ill-advised questionnaire and the overlooking of the NATED committee, who understandably resisted Maria's request to attend one of their committee meetings. It was not personal; the problem was a deep-seated mistrust of Signature. It was ironic however, that

the scheme, a qualification for CSWs that linked to the existing national occupational standards of other classroom staff
but contextualised for the CSW's specific role was actually
quite ingenious. It short-circuited the drawn-out consultation
and development of unique standards and opened the way for
a speedy resolution. However, NATED had developed standards already and held them in the 'archives'. In their view, all
that was needed was a dusting-down and a dating-up and they
would be fit for purpose. Signature were interested in seeing
them but NATED were unwilling to disclose without at least
amending them. The situation seemed like an impasse, but
Maria attended the inaugural DESF meeting as a representative
of Signature and brought people together.

DESF

It was in the months following the Derby AGM that the
Deaf Education Support Forum (DESF) was initiated, consisting of representatives of ACSW, ASLI, BATOD, NATED and
Signature, for the sharing of information, the pooling of expertise and the discussion of issues related to the education of
Deaf students of all ages. The first formal meeting took place
on 22nd June 2009 at the RNID (Royal National Institute for
Deaf People) headquarters in Central London, within a stones-
throw of John Bunyan's grave, visible from the window. The
group later expanded further and welcomed representatives
of Mary Hare Training, the Consortium of Higher Education
Support Services (CHESS), the Association of Notetaking
Professionals (ANP) and the RNID itself (thus securing the
venue for the meetings). By nature of the significance of the
collective members, it quickly commanded a reputation. Since
then, meetings have been held once every academic term.

The first challenge was to identify a national snapshot of

titles, training and qualifications of staff working in Deaf education. Andy offered to requisition and amend a question-naire devised by Vicky Nunn and used in a limited capacity by ACSW. This became the DESF Survey that eventually was published at the end of 2010.

At the first DESF meeting Maria was able to bring some agreement to factions around the table, but the process of grievance and coming to terms needed some time to run. The new CSW qualification was to be born of struggle.

CSW Qualification Struggles

In response to the imminent Signature qualification, and whilst the decision to aid the cause was pending, a small working group from the ACSW and NATED committees held a two day course-writing workshop on 20th-21st July 2009 in Derby. The work undertaken by the small band was based on historical material from the previous CSW course and the existing standards. Those involved were experienced trainers, tutors and qualified CSWs who aimed at consolidating all the legacy material and making it fit the qualification structure given by LLUK (Lifelong Learning UK) who were advising on how to write a new qualification. The working group was strongly of the opinion that CSWs should be given some train-ing on interpreting, and wrote a module specifically for that aim. The ACSW/NATED working group's aim was partly to work directly with LLUK, as an alternative to Signature, and partly to create an up-to-date viable course structure that best suited the needs of CSWs and their Deaf students.

There were complications however, because at that time, qualifications were undergoing changes. Many needed to be re-mapped to national standards, and some were due to be discontinued. It was because of this upheaval that the old CSW

Edexcel qualification finally disappeared – and there was little appetite in the industry for new qualifications. Relevant people within the qualifications industry were very difficult to get hold of, and when contact did occur there were confusing signals. The situation was on a knife-edge. It slowly became clear to those involved that something must be done quickly to prevent a national qualification for CSWs being consigned to the past. ACSW, NATED and Signature needed to work together. How this finally came about we must leave to Maria Bailey to explain in chapter 12.

Joint Conference & AGM, London 18th April 2010

On the face of it, a joint conference between ACSW and NATED seemed uncomplicated, but achieving it could have been problematic because ACSW, not yet out of school, had tied all their AGMs with a shoestring; making use of donated venues, volunteer interpreters, unpaid workshop presenters etc. NATED however were more seasoned and accustomed to charging delegate fees on a more business-like footing. In addition to this, acquiring a venue with enough space for two organisations in London involved spending some money. Greenwich University was eventually requisitioned, support professionals were commercially booked and both committees set sail hoping for a fair wind. There was some dissent from ACSW members about the hiked cost of the meeting, and an initial worry that sufficient delegates would attend, but on the day there was a good number.

Andy Owen and the NATED Chair Michelle Jones opened the conference in the historic King William Court of The Old Royal Naval College in Greenwich. The Educational Psychologist Simon Ward delivered an inspiring keynote speech and followed this up with an equally inspiring workshop. Maria

Bailey updated the conference on the Signature CSW qualification, and parried questions from the floor. It was unfortunate that some delegates were vociferous about aspects that had been through consultation way back in the initial months, but Maria was diplomatic and factual. The discussion ranged into related areas and Andy was constrained to let it take over the advertised 'Hotspot' question and answer session. Eventually it would have encroached upon lunch so had to be curtailed.

Delegates strolled to lunch between views of the Royal Observatory on the brow of the hill, and barges cutting the curve of the Thames. After the meal, other workshops included voice-over for CSWs led by Jill Newlands, a controversial presentation about voicing over profanities from Andy Owen, and a dip into an alternative code of ethics by Jason Bell. Sergeant Glen Barham MBE presented a police officer's view on mentoring Deaf teenagers and Janet Williams led a workshop on e-assessment.

The conference was a success in the face of the recent banking crisis, the decreasing availability of inexpensive venues and the education cuts beginning to effect conference attendance. The success was due largely to Hilary Hodgson of ACSW who acted as conference coordinator and made everything run as smooth as silk. It was a milestone and the ACSW committee felt that their association had somehow come of age. All that remained was for the dust to settle, the disbursements to assign and the planning to commence for the joint conference in 2011.

CSW Qualification Accredited

The new Signature qualification for CSWs was accredited just two months later in June 2010 and appeared on the Learning Aim Database. Also the application guide to National Occupation Standards for CSWs was published by LLUK. City

College Coventry became the first centre to pilot the new qualification, commencing in October 2010.

I-Sign Project Ended March 2011

On Thursday 31st March the project to develop a new formal qualification for CSWs ended. The original intention was to develop a qualification that spanned CSWs working in schools and colleges, but at the time, the Training and Development Agency for Schools (TDA) who oversaw the training for the schools sector were not able to take part in the development.

Durham Joint Conference 18th April 2011

The joint conference between ACSW and NATED the previous year was going to be a hard act to follow. Michelle Jones, NATED Chair, stepped up to the mark with a little help from her friends. At that meeting, Jill Newlands took over the ACSW Chair role and Andy Owen stepped into a newly opened role of Vice Chair, thereby commencing his final year on the committee since it's conception in 2006. Vicky Nunn remained as Treasurer, Nigel Kerwin joined as Secretary, and Miriam Marchi as Membership Secretary. Three new posts were created: Ricci Collins as Deaf Link Officer, Jess Clover as Volunteer Co-ordinator and Bob Blackwell as Fundraising Officer.

Keynote presentations were by Maria Bailey, who updated conference on the Signature CSW qualification, I-Sign and other developments, and Tessa Padden, who offered some personal thoughts on communication support and sign language interpreting for Deaf learners in education. A workshop was led by Linda Richards who explored the place of translation in interpreting, and how an early introduction to translation studies can transform interpreter training and practice. Jill Newlands presented a workshop for the second year running on voiceover, and explored some of the difficulties faced when interpreting from BSL into English in the classroom. Melanie Thorley of the Association of Notetaking Professionals presented a workshop on the who, why, what, where and when of Notetakers. A workshop was led by Rachel O'Neill, who asked, 'What qualifications are there to learn how to modify language successfully?'. Rachel explored examples of texts modified for exams and for classroom materials, and discussed issues arising when working with examination boards. A final workshop was presented by Rachael Hayes and Tim Richardson of National Deaf CAMHS (Child and Adolescent Mental Health Service) and covered an introduction to the service, referral procedure and joint working. At the conference Linda Richards donated a free CSW mentoring opportunity in a prize-draw. Angela Fenney was chosen at random from all the entrants, and Linda duly visited Angela who is a CSW in Manchester.

Although feedback from the conference was positive, attendance was lower than in previous years, with all areas of life feeling the financial pinch. In the year leading up to the next conference in 2012, the idea for this book was germinated. Also in 2012 Andy led the work of writing a proposal for opening a category for CSWs in the NRCPD (The National Registers for Communication Professionals working with Deaf and Deafblind People). This involved not only gaining the support of the ACSW and NATED committees, but also the members of the DESF, comprising representatives of Action on Hearing Loss (formerly RNID), the Association of Notetaking Professionals (ANP), the Association of Sign Language Interpreters (ASLI), the British Association of Teachers of the Deaf (BATOD), the Consortium of Higher Education Support Services with Deaf Students (CHESS), Mary Hare Training and Signature. It was an historic step, and represented a meeting of minds of all stakeholders involved in the education of Deaf learners, all supporting the proposal that a category in the NRCPD be opened for CSWs – CSW Registration. The proposal comprised a 70 page document and was formally presented to the NRCPD on the 15th of February 2012 for discussion at its board meeting the following March. At that March meeting, the issue was briefly discussed, but was rescheduled as a substantive agenda item for the board's July 2012 meeting, the discussion to be aimed at how to proceed with a view to securing a wide range of views on the impact of regulating CSWs, and the role that NRCPD might play in that.

Because that meeting was scheduled to take place after the publication of this volume, it means that we are unable to report with any closure on the matter, so the issue will continue.

12
The I-Sign Project

The DCSF (Department for Children, Schools and Families) funded I-Sign Project ran for two years, between 2009 and 2011. It's overall aim was:

'To improve BSL provision and status for families of Deaf and hearing impaired children'

The project was piloted in two geographical areas, North West and South West England, with the aim to roll out across the UK. Stakeholders included Deaf children, their families, the children's workforce, teachers and interpreters

The project had a number of consortium members:

- RNID (Royal National Institute for Deaf People)
- NDCS (National Deaf Children's Society)
- BDA (British Deaf Association)
- Signature
- UCLAN (University of Central Lancashire)

- Exeter Academy of Deaf Education (ERADE).
- Merseyside Society for Deaf People.

Each member of the consortium led on different elements of the project. The final report and evaluation, with recommendations of future developments is reprinted below, thanks to kind permission from the consortium members. We considered this to be such an important and informative body of work that we wanted to reproduce it in its entirety.

I-SIGN Project Evaluation and recommendations on future developments for children whose first language is BSL

Recommendations on future developments.
March 2011

I-Sign and the need for a continuing focus on language acquisition by Deaf children, supported by their families and professionals.

Summary

I-Sign was developed in response to the recognition that there is a weak infrastructure and no consistent support, to ensure that Deaf children born to hearing families can easily acquire full and confident language ability. The issue can effectively be addressed through supporting parents and professionals within the school system to increase their skills in British Sign Language (BSL) This requires addressing family needs and securing better training and support of professionals within the school and further and higher education systems. As a result of the geographical spread of BSL use and high level of language skills needed, we must ensure that there is a developed infrastructure of language support and tutor training to deliver BSL capacity.

This is not currently available across the UK. I-Sign has been very successful in piloting programmes and work practices that have tackled these issues.

I-Sign was a pilot to develop BSL capacity in two contrasting regions (North West and South West England), the summary outputs from the project were:

116 families accessed family sign language courses

73 people achieved full BSL qualifications at Levels 3 or 4

6 people achieved part qualification at Levels 3 and 4

16 new interpreters achieved registered status

2 existing interpreters achieved the intermediate status

5 existing interpreters achieved full qualification and 'member' registration status

1 existing interpreter achieved part qualification

18 Deaf people undertook professional development via formal teacher training

10 existing Deaf teachers undertook professional development via a course specific programme

114 existing Deaf teachers accessed continual professional development events

12 interpreters and Deaf teachers achieved qualifications that enable them to deliver NVQs

Web and DVD based family sign language resources were created with 7951 unique visitors to the website and 741 DVDs sent out (by February 2011).

A new qualification of Level 3 Certificate in Learning Support (Communication Support Worker) was developed and is currently being piloted.

The challenge which remains is how to ensure the long term viability of language support, without long-term central government investment.

The importance of the work done by I-Sign and the need for this to continue, reflects the compelling evidence that without better support for language acquisition by Deaf children, through helping to support their hearing parents and professionals, these children will continue to fail. This failure is not only in terms of educational outcomes but also wider social and emotional development, leading to poor qualifications, poor employment prospects, increased mental health problems during the school years, and increased risk of committing crime in later life. Moreover, support to gain language is a human rights issue, recognised in International Conventions to which the UK Government is a signatory. Work to address this is expected by International and UK law around discrimination, which forms part of the underpinning for the Department for Education to meet its aims to improve outcomes for children with SEN.

In order to address these issues there is a continuing need to invest in the development of national capacity to ensure that the current gains of the programme are not lost. This is particularly relevant at the current time given the rearrangement of funding vehicles with an ever smaller geographical focus. The actions that we suggest need to be taken are summarised as;

Recommendation 1

There is a need to provide language support for children and young people who are Deaf, both within the family and in educational settings, to facilitate effective language acquisition. This foundation is necessary for full access, and equality of potential attainment.

This need is already supported by international conventions on the rights of the child, and in UK Equalities, Education and Health legislation. However, to support this in practice Government should;

a. Consider establishing specific statutory guidance on the requirement to provide adequate language support in family services, early years settings, schools and further and higher education. This could be achieved through either revision of existing legislation or the creation of new regulations flowing from the Green Paper reforms,

b. Ensure that specific guidance is developed to supplement existing early support and Sure Start provision for families.

c. Concurrently to the considerations on statutory guidance; make clearer to schools their specific responsibilities to provide high quality language support. This could be achieved through guidance which supports the implementation of existing legislation and would also help guide how the new extension of Auxiliary Aids will be addressed;

Recommendation 2

That the Department of Education explores with I-Sign the creation of a nationally funded language support resource. The resource would act as the support and catalyst for the development of local capacity and underpin local training. This framework will ensure the delivery of a minimum standard of language support for Deaf children and young people, and advise and support families and professionals through best practice. Whilst this would need some initial funding; the goal would be that this national resource would duly become self-supporting through fees from local agencies, schools and local training income.

Recommendation 3

That as part of the review of the integration of pre and post 16 entitlements and provision, including the establishment of a new education plan, the Department reviews language support provision for young learners. The current system, as shown by lack of attainment, is failing them.

The I-Sign Consortium would like to meet with the Department to explore how these ideas could continue the progress made through the project to date, to establish a national framework of guidance with the capacity to become self-funding over time.

Context

Numbers of Deaf children.

In the UK, there are about 20,000 children aged 0-15 who are moderately to profoundly Deaf. About 12,000 of these were born Deaf, with about one in every 1,000 children being Deaf at three years of age. This rises to two in every 1,000 children aged nine to 16. Of these, an estimated 840 children are born in the UK every year with moderate to profound Deafness. Causes include genetic factors (50%), intrauterine (8%), perinatal (12%), and postnatal (30%). There is no definite, known aetiology for 20-30% of Deaf children (Fortnum, Sommerfield et al, 2001). Deaf children are also at increased risk of additional disabilities; as well as dual sensory disorders, learning disabilities, and physical disabilities. As a consequence of being Deaf in a hearing orientated world Deaf children and adults are also at an increased risk from mental health problems.

Deaf Children in Education

Figures from the School Census

According to 2009 figures from the Department for Education, there are 15,520 Deaf children in England. Of these:

* 6,420 have a statement of special educational needs (SEN) under the SEN Code of Practice (41%)
* 9,100 have been placed at School Action Plus under the SEN Code of Practice (59%)

However, these figures do not include Deaf children who are at School Action only under the SEN Code of Practice or who have not been formally recorded as having a SEN. The figures also exclude children where Deafness is not the primary type of SEN (i.e. those who have more severe needs, such as learning disabilities).

Figures from Local Authorities

According to an NDCS survey of local authorities in 2009 (which received responses from 144 local authorities), there are at least 27,800 Deaf children of school age in England. This suggests that the Department's figures underestimate the number of Deaf children by around half.

The Importance of Communication

'language is what makes thought possible' (Joseph Church).

Language acquisition is something that is often taken for granted but is, in essence, fundamental to the functioning of a person and the ability to gain language must therefore be seen as a fundamental human right. We take language acquisition for granted in most children but for children whose first language is not spoken English but British Sign Language we cannot assume the normal pattern of language acquisition within the family will happen. Further, this is then compounded by the lack of professional understanding and support within the early years and schools context.

New research has highlighted the importance of learning a

language, whether signed or spoken, early in life. 'Early acquisition of a first language is critical not only for processing that language, but also appears to form a base on which subsequently learned languages can successfully build.' (Woll, 2008)

Behavioural studies have demonstrated the importance of ensuring that a first language (whether spoken or signed) is developed at the age appropriate time. Skills in communication have been shown by various studies to correlate highly with positive outcomes, including language development, reading skills, and social-emotional development.

Most profoundly Deaf children are born into a unique linguistic situation according to Mitchell and Karchmer (2004). Hearing loss prevents them from acquiring the naturally-occurring, spoken language of their parents with nine out of every ten Deaf children born to hearing parents. Without access to language, they are unable to fully participate in the family interactions that are so crucial to language development. Work by Gregory et al (1995) and Ratna also estimated that 81% of parents of Deaf children never learn how to communicate with their Deaf child. Calderon (2000) examined outcomes for Deaf children in an early intervention programme in terms of what were good predictors of successful language acquisition. Factors included: level of the child's hearing loss, mother's educational level, mother's current communication skills with her child and maternal use of additional services beyond those offered by the intervention programme. Thus pointing to the crucial role played by additional support and development of communication skills in language acquisition.

Children who are Deaf are at a high risk for delays in communication and language development, poor academic achievement, delays in critical thinking skills, and problems with social and emotional development due to the central role that language plays in these essential areas as argued by Rall

(2007). They are also more at risk of ending up in the criminal justice system in part due to communication issues developed during parental socialisation. Gregory, Bishop and Sheldon (1995) also paint a depressing picture of families under stress, where Deaf young people, unable to hear the conversation of the family, are not fully participating in society or family life. It is not surprising in these circumstances that Deaf children then face a multiplicity of problems that impact on education and life skills.

Children whose parents had poor communication skills have also been shown to have greater behaviour problems. This suggests that parents who focus efforts on developing strong communication skills reduce the risk of having children with social and emotional difficulties, as well as improving reading skills and language development.

Poor communication between Deaf children and their parents also leads to greater mental health problems; this was acknowledged in the 1970s through the work of the John Denmark Centre. Wallis et al. (2004) specifically defined effective communication as one in which parents and children share the same communication mode (both using English, or both using sign language). Using adolescent self-reports, they found that mismatch between language modes was a significant correlate of mental health functioning. Those with sign mismatch (an adolescent using sign language, parents using spoken language) had the lowest mental health functioning. Those with spoken match (adolescent and parents both using spoken language) had higher ratings, while Deaf adolescents of Deaf parents showed the healthiest functioning of all categories. For the UK, Hindley et al. (1994) report prevalence rates of 31% in Deaf children, in comparison to an estimated prevalence of 20% for hearing peers.

Impact on Attainment

'It has been recognised for over 30 years that Deaf children of Deaf parents generally have improved educational outcomes compared to Deaf children of hearing parents.'(Woll, 2008) In that context, ensuring that there is adequate language support for children born into hearing families and that professionals can then further their language acquisition and properly support their access to the curriculum, is crucial. Further studies show that parental involvement and good language support are the two key determinates of what helps Deaf children become successful (Powers, 2006).

There continues to be a serious lack of good research about the attainment outcomes for Deaf children whose first language is BSL. More generally we know that the overall performance of Deaf and hard of hearing children falls significantly behind their hearing peers (SEN, 2010) However this figure is an aggregate of the whole range of hearing loss and it is likely therefore that Deaf children dependant on BSL as their first language will be performing below this level.

Studies over the years have shown the marked delays in the language, educational and reading attainments of profoundly Deaf children (Conrad, Blamey et al, 1979) It is well established that the teaching of children with BSL as their first language needs not only specialist methods but also good language skills from support staff. Moreover we know from all studies of parental involvement that parents being involved in the education of their children has a significant impact on the commitment and achievements of their children, generally, but especially where SEN is concerned (Lamb, 2009)

The issues for Deaf children and young people continue within their post 16 education. LSC data indicates that Deaf students were underrepresented on all but level one courses. In the 2007/8 academic year there were 39% fewer Deaf students on level three courses than on level one courses. For those with visual impairment the decrease was only 7%. For non-disabled students the numbers actually increased by 180%. Deaf students from BME backgrounds face additional challenges. There were 86% fewer Deaf students from Afro and Afro-Caribbean backgrounds on level 3 than level 1 courses. (Bridging the Access Gap conference, 2008).

The impact of this situation cannot be underestimated both in human and economic terms. Some studies estimate that every extra year in education beyond 16 is worth an 8% increase in annual pay as well as benefits associated with improved mental and physical health and wellbeing for the young person and their family. RNID research shows that 63% of Deaf people are currently in employment (RNID, 2006) compared to 75% of the general population (Labour Force Survey, 2008), 57% of Deaf people had been looking for work for more than 12 months, this compared to only 20% of the total of unemployed people at the time (Brien, Brown and Collins, 2002).

Deaf Children's Views

Within education, Deaf children also reflect that the quality of the support they receive is directly related to their educational achievement. NDCS conducted an online poll of Deaf children and young people on 'The Buzz', their youth website. 70 Deaf children responded, and:

94% say that it is easier to do well at school when they get special help BUT

Nearly 60% say that they only get some help or that the help they get is not enough.

National Service Context

I-Sign has had some notable successes through piloting a range of different delivery models. It has also highlighted some striking deficiencies in the provision for Deaf children. As such, it is in a good place to make recommendations on how we can address the shortcomings in existing services for Deaf children. Despite a number of improvements since the 2002 report, commissioned by the then Department for Work and Pensions, to the overall provision and professional structure of BSL interpreting services, these are still patchy, often not provided to the appropriate standard, especially in school settings and training and opportunities to learn are still focused in centres of excellence and some adult learning centres.

I-Sign has sought to address some of these shortfalls; its successes have been built on the foundations of public sector services for Deaf children and these are being eroded. HE cuts are leading to universities rejecting Deaf students as they are too expensive. LA cuts are reducing the specialist support staff available to support Deaf children in mainstream education, and the ones that remain have no CPD budget to pay for their training needs. Cuts to early years provision are significantly threatening the possibility of any funding to support the family sign language curriculum courses. There is a real danger that the investment made in I-Sign may be wasted because the public sector cuts will mean the programmes, courses, qualifications and services developed will not be funded by schools, colleges, universities and other public sector bodies. Further we are aware that much language support within the classroom is already not at the level necessary to support children accessing the curriculum in an adequate way even when it is available.

The national service context is also complex with very significant changes taking place in the overall structure of educational provision with the introduction of Academies and Free Schools with delegated SEN budgets to those schools, more power and decision making being devolved to head teachers and a major revision of the SEN Framework. The major concern for such a low incidence group as children with BSL as their first language will be that with delegation of resources and responsibility there will be even less incentives in the system for a co-ordinated approach for such a low incidence group. Language users' needs are already a low priority within the system and the danger is that they slip further.

Building on the I-Sign investment - potential for future developments

Children have a fundamental right to be able to access education. This is well established in international and domestic legislation. Without parents having the language support and skills to communicate with their children, and without schools and support staff having the ability to communicate with children who have BSL as their first language, then this fundamental right is effectively being denied.

The Need to Create a Core Offer for Children with BSL as their first language

There are a number of legislative requirements and policy developments around the provision of SEN and disability that suggest now is a good time to consider establishing a core offer with minimum standards in provision for children with BSL as their first language.

International Law

There are a number of articles from the UN Convention on

Human Rights, to which the UK is a signatory, which are relevant to this issue; including Article 9 on Accessibility, Article 23 on the Family and especially Article 24 on Education which states;

> 'States Parties shall enable persons with disabilities to learn life and social development skills to facilitate their full and equal participation in education and as members of the community. To this end, States Parties shall take appropriate measures, including:
>
> Facilitating the learning of sign language and the promotion of the linguistic identity of the Deaf community;
>
> Ensuring that the education of persons, and in particular children, who are blind, Deaf or Deafblind, is delivered in the most appropriate languages and modes and means of communication for the individual, and in environments which maximize academic and social development.
>
> In order to help ensure the realization of this right, States Parties shall take appropriate measures to employ teachers, including teachers with disabilities, who are qualified in sign language and/or Braille, and to train professionals and staff who work at all levels of education. Such training shall incorporate disability awareness and the use of appropriate augmentative and alternative modes, means and formats of communication, educational techniques and materials to support persons with disabilities.'

The UK Government is a signatory to this agreement but the requirements of the Act are not specifically encapsulated within legislation directly, though there are a number of areas of UK legislation that are key to delivery of these obligations, especially the Equality Act 2010 where, subject to the requirements of reasonable accommodation, service providers, including schools and further and high education institutions, would have responsibilities to ensure that BSL support is provided to access services.

UK Legislation

SEND Framework

The 1966 Education Act and the resulting SEN framework, supplemented by the Equality Act 2010, provide the framework for educational provision for children whose first language is BSL. Children with BSL as their first language would fall under both the SEN and Disability definitions.

The SEN Framework makes clear that children who are identified as having a special educational need by being placed on school action, school action plus or are the subject of a Statement of Special Educational Needs should then be provided with the support necessary for their educational needs to be met. Most of this group of children are likely to be statemented or identified through the SEN framework. Where language support is identified as part of the statement, this should be provided. However, with only 25 % of Deaf children having a statement, we cannot rely on simply the assessment process to identify and deliver all the necessary language support and even when children are being statemented and language support provided; it may often not be to the standard necessary to support adequate communication and learning.

Children Act 1989

This Act requires Local Authorities to identify the extent to which children are in need in their area and provide services designed to minimise the effect of their disabilities and to give them the opportunity to lead as normal lives as possible. One of the main assessment mechanisms is the Common Assessment Framework which is designed to help professional staff across a range of services to record and share assessments plans and

244 History of Communication Support Workers

recommendations. Guidance requires that such assessments should focus on the particular needs of the child including educational and language needs. Deaf children are children in need as defined by the Children Act 1989.

Equality Act 2010

As well as the general duty to provide reasonable accommodations in respect of education services and the public duty on schools in relation to promoting Equality, the Act extends the requirement to provide auxiliary aids to education services, following from a recommendation in the Lamb Inquiry which will come into force in Autumn 2011. The draft guidance clearly states that schools will be responsible for auxiliary aids including;

7.15 A school must take such steps as it is reasonable for them to have to take, to provide auxiliary aids so as to avoid the disadvantage experienced by disabled pupils.

What is an auxiliary aid?

7.16 An auxiliary aid includes an auxiliary service and is anything which provides additional support or assistance to a disabled pupil. Examples include:

- a piece of equipment;
- the provision of a sign language interpreter, lip-speaker or Deaf-blind communicator
- extra staff assistance for disabled pupils
- an electronic or manual note-taking service
- an induction loop or infrared broadcast system
- videophones
- audio-visual fire alarms.

The New Green Paper Proposals

Support and aspiration: A new approach to special educational needs and disability. Department for Education (2011)

The Green Paper envisages a number of reforms that impact on the future provision of language support for families and professionals. The main areas are;

- Assessment and early intervention from birth
- Integrated Health and Education Plan to replace the Statement
- Development of professional expertise on SEN with teachers and support staff
- Parents having much greater say over the way in which budgets related to special education provision are controlled by parents.
- The expansion of Achievement for All as the main mechanism within mainstream education for addressing outcome issues
- A 'Local Offer' of provision which make clear what the entitlements at local level would be, with clearer information and greater transparency
- More unified provision between pre and post 16 years.

Many of these objectives will not be realisable for Deaf children without the language support and infrastructure that the I-Sign project has begun to put in place. For example, it is difficult to see how the aim of allowing parents to purchase vital support for their children's development would work for language support unless there is a developed market of trained communication support workers and interpreters with the required level of qualifications. The Local Offer will not work for this group of parents if authorities do not focus on the language issue; they will need support in doing this given the very low incidence but high level of needs of this group. Further, the development of teacher expertise and specialist support in classrooms and other settings will not take place at the appropriate standard, nor will there be the necessary expertise available, without further development.

While in time, a viable market may appear in some areas as authorities and schools focus on this, the fact that responsibility is being dispersed over the next few years as a consequence of the devolution of budgets and responsibilities to Heads, development of academies and free schools and great freedoms locally all suggest the need for some initial pump priming of expertise and a national framework to allow this to take place.

A Core Offer with Minimum Standards

Both existing legislative requirements and the development of the new duty around auxiliary aids create a powerful set of obligations for early years services, schools, colleges and higher education to support pupils whose first language is not English. Further there is an appropriate emphasis on bringing the knowledge and expertise of parents more into the system and Achievement for All depends on the ability of parents as part of the structured conversation.

We know that both parents and professionals will struggle unless there are some clearer guidelines about what is good practice in this area, how to go about acquiring language skills for yourself and your child if you are a parent and how to ensure that you are providing the appropriate support, advice and correct level of communication support if you are a teacher or related professional. It is clear there are major issues in the delivery of sign language support due to a lack of well qualified interpreters, lack of awareness of the appropriate qualification of those providing sign language support and lack of support for parents to acquire the necessary language skills.

Further with a more devolved system, and the very low incidence nature of BSL usage, it is very unlikely local services will be in a position to respond well without additional support and guidance. By building on the work of I-Sign we believe that local capacity can be supported to the standard required for schools to address the duty.

Recommendation 1

There is a need to provide language support for children and young people who are Deaf, both within the family and in educational settings, to facilitate effective language acquisition. This foundation is necessary for full access, and equality of potential attainment. To achieve this Government should;

a. Consider if it is necessary to establish more specific statutory guidance either through revision of existing legislation or the creation of new regulations flowing from the Green Paper reforms on the requirement to provide adequate language support in family services, early years setting, schools and further and higher education,

b. Ensure that specific guidance is developed, supplementing existing early support and Sure Start provision for families.

c. While considering the long term need for new legislation, make clearer to schools their specific responsibilities to provide high quality language support through specific through guidance which supports the implementation of existing legislation and also helps guide how the new extension of Auxiliary Aids will be addressed;

Guidance could both summarise existing legislative requirements and also reflect best practice standards. It could form a very helpful addition to the guidance on reasonable accommodation and the new requirements in the Equality Act 2010 on provision of Auxiliary Aids where, out of necessity, the standard guidance will be brief.

This would provide the overall context for delivery of support and be a helpful resource for providers and also guide parents who are thinking of commissioning their own support under the new arrangements. This would be especially relevant given the devolution of commissioning of specialist support services in the case of Academies and Free Schools.

As part of a national guidance it would be important to align this with the development of professional skills in the workforce as envisaged in the Green Paper on SEN and Disabled Children. There are a number of levels this would be relevant to but in the light of the I-Sign work, it would especially be worth examining a specialist training module for Learning Support Assistants and teaching assistants to support the implementation of this approach.

It would also be worth looking at how the lessons learnt from integrating the I-Sign approach with early years settings could be developed further, not least by ensuring that the support that is developed at this stage could be taken up the age range with the children as they progress. Again there are some analogies here as to how Early Support Programme model has been moved up the age range in some LA's practice with disabled and SEN children. This early intervention approach is also entirely consistent with the approach outlined in the Green Paper and could be combined with the early assessment which is now envisaged, providing support for the language acquisition component. One option is to consider how the joint plan which replaces the statement could look at a more joined up approach across children's and education services and it may well be worth considering how this could be piloted as one of the proposed Government pilots of the new assessment.

The I-Sign consortium would value an opportunity to discuss these possible models further with the department.

Recommendation 2

The Department of Education explores with I-Sign the setting up of a nationally funded resource to support the delivery of a minimum standard of language support and best practice with families and professionals, to act as the support and catalyst for the development of local capacity, and also to support training and advice to parents and professionals. The aim would be that this resource would eventually become self-supporting through fees from local agencies and schools and local training resources.

Supporting Local Delivery

While establishing a clearer national framework there also needs to be provision for a central or regional resource which can effect some economies of scale in providing central resources, bridges the gaps in current practice between Department of Education and Department for Business, Innovation and Skills around support issues, and becomes a catalyst for better provision and the development of local services and support in line with minimum standards.

The core elements that the national resource could deliver would include;

- Supporting the development of local expertise and centres of excellence, that in turn support capacity growth in sign language support, along the lines pioneered by the I-Sign project,
- Support the development and delivery of specialist training courses in sign language at different levels to support the growth of sign language capacity within schools and the community including interpreter training,
- Support the development of family support workers and family sign courses to ensure that language acquisition can be supported within the family. Support families coming to terms with the language and culture issues involved and help create improved links between families and schools,

enabling parents to better support children in education.

- Continue to develop and support national standards of excellence and be a central resource for Government and local agencies to help support the raising of standards and the profile of the issue to service providers and support the involvement of parents and driving up outcomes for Deaf children.

In time, in each region, the aim would be to ensure that service providers could demonstrate competence in supporting language acquisition in a number of settings. This work would ideally also bring together different agencies across education and health as envisaged by the Green Paper for children who are statemented under the new assessment plan.

What is important, is to establish the principles that such a resource is needed, rather than trying to be too prescriptive about the precise form of the models for delivery. However there are a number of examples where the department has worked closely with the sector to effect supported change in some key areas, without being too prescriptive about the means. One of the most obvious examples being the Early Support Programme which used a central resource of producing specialist advice and standards linked to enhancing training capacity and local support. A step further could be to create a national centre (virtual or physical) to promote the development of nationally consistent standards but be the catalyst for local development of capacity and support as described above and we have illustrated how this might be developed in Appendix 1.

Recommendation 3

That as part of the Department's review of the integration of pre and post 16 entitlements and provision, including the establishment of a new education plan to replace the statement and access to training, further and higher education, the department reviews the functioning of language support for young learners which is currently failing them.

While in theory, post 16 provision has a number of statutory entitlements which should ensure Deaf learners have the language support they need, we know in practice that this is often lacking due to poor infrastructure, lack of funds and access to suitably qualified interpreters, even where funds are available. As part of the Department's review of post 16 provision flagged in the Green Paper we would want to explore how we better embed language support in any new arrangements.

The I-Sign Consortium would like to meet with the department to explore how these ideas could continue the progress made through the project to date and establish a national framework of guidance and capacity to support its delivery, with capacity to become self-funding over time.

Conclusion

I-Sign has provided a solid basis to explore and develop approaches towards language acquisition for children whose first language is BSL, ensuring that they are able to participate better in school and improve social and academic functioning by ensuring both parents and schools and colleges have the expertise and support to help children acquire language and all that goes with this. However, without a sustained and continuing focus on this issue, with some central support and infrastructure support, it is highly likely that the developments and innovations that have been supported through the programme will end. Worse, with the sustained cut backs now taking place across early years, schools, college and higher education, children and young adults' participation is likely to decline not increase.

We do not envisage large additional investment from central government but without some additional financial support that would allow a co-ordinated approach and for the voluntary sector to have the capacity to leverage further funding through local sources, it is difficult to see how the gains of the last two years will not go to waste.

Appendix 1

One possible Model-National Centre

Development of a National social enterprise model to deliver the type of service that I-Sign has been piloting.

An answer is to create a National Centre for Sign Language Education. This will have a responsibility for ensuring that each region has the capacity to deliver the key services, courses and qualification for those who work and live with Deaf children and so enable Deaf children to fulfil their potential.

Part of its remit is therefore to audit existing providers and to identify where new agencies are needed. Each region would need:

- FSLC capability
- BSL teaching centre for staff who work with Deaf children
- ECSW teaching centre for staff who work with Deaf children (0-19)
- Teaching qualifications delivered for Deaf people to ensure enough BSL tutors are trained to meet the demand for BSL courses

There would also need to be a minimum entitlement for Deaf children (ECSW with BSL L3 and ECSW qualification for example). This would need to be funded through a national funding stream, rather than expecting schools, colleges, LAs, HE to fund the necessary support for students through existing funding, as that doesn't work. This could be established as a Social Enterprise, established by I-Sign partners, which is pump primed by the Departments of Education, Health and Business Innovation and Skills.

If constructed as a social enterprise this would lock any assets to the further development of the service, and enable it to trade. The centre needs to facilitate the establishment of social enterprises to develop new projects (regional ECSW services for example), which should be self-funding as they could deliver higher quality service than current LA/FE provision and thus can win contracts from LAs etc, who will hire them in preference to running the service themselves. The Centre's job would be to identify agencies that can deliver programmes, or develop capacity of regions to do the same.

Creating a centre provides a visual signal that there is a dedicated education resource for sign language using Deaf children. One of the learning outcomes of I-Sign is that the needs of Deaf student can get lost in big organisations, because there aren't enough of them to get noticed. A specialist social enterprise ensures that won't happen. Further, by making this independent and delivered from within the voluntary sector it is meeting the department's desire to bring the voluntary sector more centrally into the co-ordination of assessment as envisaged by the White Paper and there may be possibilities of using this to pilot some of the ideas around joint assessment as envisaged in the Green Paper.

Funding could be based on similar model to National Deaf CAMHS service -national centre with regional hubs. It could administer tenders for work to enable the minimum entitlement to be offered, or the minimum entitlement could be done through personalised budgets and the role of the centre would be to make sure there are the services and support available for Deaf students to buy.

I-Sign Project Update April 2012

Discussions have been ongoing with DFE since the end of the project; the current economic climate means that finances are not currently available (April 2012) for roll out of the project nationally. The I-Sign consortium is exploring with DFE the possibility of discrete pieces of capacity building work at this time.

Report

Development of Signature Level 3 Certificate for Communication Support Workers as part of the DCSF (Department for Children, Schools and Families) funded I Sign Project.

The appointment of Maria Bailey as the I Sign Project Officer for Signature in 2009 can be described as an example of serendipity. Although Maria was not seeking the appointment, indeed was unaware of the plans for the development of a new qualification for communication support workers (CSWs) or of the I Sign Project itself at the time, the opportunity simply presented itself and she willingly accepted the challenge.

In March 2009 Maria received an unexpected email from Cathy Barnes of Signature, tentatively asking whether she would be interested in undertaking some work on behalf of Signature, which would involve researching and developing a new qualification for CSWs. Signature had recently changed their name from CACDP (Council for the Advancement of Communication with Deaf People). Maria was intrigued because she had met Cathy some years earlier whilst working as a Course Leader for City of Sunderland College, but had no contact with her since. A meeting soon took place and all became clear.

Setting the Scene

Maria was working as a CSW at New College Durham. Having returned from a three year spell of living in Spain between 2004 and 2007, she had decided that she no longer wanted the stress of working in management in further education, but would still like to be involved in Deaf education. Word soon spread around the Deaf grapevine that Maria had returned from Spain and, after a brief three month spell of working with a Deaf student at Newcastle College, she was soon invited to join the Sensory Support team at New College, Durham. Maria duly started working there in September 2007. One of Maria's colleagues at New College, Wendy Martin, a Teacher of the Deaf who has long links with CACDP/ Signature, had been given the post of CSW Officer for a short time until funding ran out. Wendy had recommended Maria to Signature as someone who might be willing and able to undertake the work involved.

At that first meeting in Signature's office in Durham, it was explained that Signature were part of a consortium that had been granted funding from a government funded project, the I Sign Project. The project had an overall aim of improving British Sign Language (BSL) provision for Deaf children and their families. A full report of the project is included earlier in this Chapter. One of the strands of the project that Signature had responsibility for was to research and develop a new qualification for 'Educational Communication Support Workers.' The project had started in March 2009 and was to last for two years. The work sounded both challenging and satisfying. Maria accepted the offer and started work immediately, admittedly with a mixture of apprehension and excitement. Already she sensed the importance of the work and the impact that it could have. She questioned her own ability, but always willing to accept a challenge, was keen to test her limits and hopefully achieve something worthwhile.

Stakeholder Contact

The first task was to make contact with various stakeholders including employers, the current CSW workforce, Deaf students, voluntary organisations and the two Sector Skills Councils (SSCs) who controlled qualifications in the education sector at that time. The two SSCs were the TDA (Training and Development Agency for Schools) who controlled qualifications in the schools sector and LLUK (Lifelong Learning UK) who controlled qualifications in the Post Compulsory/ Further Education (FE) sector. This all sounded a little daunting at first, but feeling confident about the expected outcome and with assurance of receiving excellent guidance, the journey commenced at the beginning of April 2009.

Questionnaire Not Well Received

In March 2009, a questionnaire had been circulated to working CSWs via Andy Owen, who at that time was the National Chair of ACSW (Association of Communication Support Workers). Unfortunately this was not well received due to the nature of the questions and how they had been presented. A NATED (the National Association for Tertiary Education for Deaf People) representative soon made contact to ask why they had not received the questionnaires. It transpired that they had been inadvertently omitted from the circulation. There were a lot of people on the warpath. It was not a good place to start. Unknowingly, Maria was walking into a storm that would take time and a lot of soothing of tempers to overcome.

The overriding concern about the proposed development of a new qualification for CSWs lay in the fact that LLUK already had a core qualification for Learning Support Practitioners. They were slowly liaising with a number of organisations and encouraging the development of 'specialist' pathways within the qualification. LLUK were supportive of the suggestion that Signature develop such a pathway for CSWs, but the title of the qualification would need to be 'Level 3 Certificate in Learning Support (Communication Support Worker). There was a great reluctance to accept the term 'Learning Support' in a new qualification for CSWs. Understandably, CSWs had struggled long and hard to be accepted as professionals in their own right, not as Support Assistants or Teaching Assistants. It took a long time and a lot of persuasion for people to accept that it was the content of the qualification that was most important, not the title. LLUK explained quite clearly, that in their view there were qualifications for those who lead the learning, and qualifications for the workforce who assist with, or support the learning, under the guidance of someone else, hence the title 'Learning Support Practitioner.' A learning support practitioner supports learning as opposed to leading the learning. This proved to be an enormous hurdle to overcome. Maria remembers feeling a little stunned and confused at the reactions she received, and did not see how she could continue with the development in the face of such resistance and negativity. However, a breath of fresh air soon presented itself.

ERADE

The Exeter Royal Academy of Deaf Education (ERADE) were one of the partners in the I Sign Consortium. Soon after embarking on the project, Maria was contacted by Jane Godwin, the CSW Manager at ERADE to ask if she could be of any assistance. Keen to make progress, an initial meeting was quickly arranged. Prior to the meeting Maria had sent Jane a copy of the LLUK Level 3 qualification specification for Learning Support Practitioners. Maria had already read this and felt that much of the content was appropriate for CSW training. She was confident that by developing some additional units relative to CSWs, it should possible to create a specialist pathway, thereby developing an appropriate qualification for CSWs. Jane was asked to read the LLUK material, disregarding the overall title, or even the title of the units. The main question was whether in her opinion, the content was suitable for CSW training. That initial meeting took place on 22 June 2009 in London. Jane proved to be a true ally after Maria had experienced months of struggle and negativity. Jane stated that she believed the LLUK course content was indeed suitable for CSW training. She was so confident, calm and supportive. This was what was desperately needed. At the time Jane was training CSWs at ERADE using an OCN (Open College Network) qualification that had been adapted to match the needs of ERADE and their CSW workforce. She agreed that most of the content of the OCN course could easily be adapted to match the LLUK content. This news was extremely welcome and gave Maria renewed confidence in the proposal. It became clear that the planned development of a specialist pathway to the existing LLUK qualification was indeed possible. The next task now was to convince everyone else.

Reluctance to Cooperate

As part of the development process, research was needed to prove that there was a demand for CSW training and that any development could be sustainable. Contact had already been made with NATED and ACSW, although they were somewhat reluctant to cooperate at the time. Paul Simpson of BATOD (British Association of Teachers of the Deaf) had been contacted to discuss the development. Paul was very sympathetic and offered his support. He explained that representatives of various organisations had been meeting regularly to discuss issues concerning the education of Deaf students. The meetings were held in London at the RNID (Royal National

Institute for Deaf People, now known as Action on Hearing Loss). Maria was invited to attend the next meeting, scheduled to take place on 22 June 2009. This proved to be a pivotal date in the research stage. Representatives from BATOD, NATED, ACSW and ASLI (Association of Sign Language Intrepreters) were in attendance, in addition to Andrew Burgess, Head of the Sensory Service (HoSS) at Greenwich, London. At that meeting, the development of the CSW qualification within the I Sign project was outlined. Paul Simpson asked Maria what those present could do to help. The response was simple 'Work with me, not against me.' Grievances were aired and an understanding was reached. From that point support was forthcoming from all colleagues and any negativity quickly evaporated. It was at that same meeting that the members present decided that they should form an official forum. Hence the DESF (Deaf Education Support Forum) was born. Further information on the DESF can be found in Chapter 15. DESF meetings have continued to be held three times per year, each term. Sincere thanks must go to members of DESF whose help was invaluable in the early research phase of the CSW development. Their contacts were crucial to the work that was taking place and a broader range of people were consulted than would otherwise have been possible.

Sadly, one obstacle that proved impossible to overcome, was the desire to create one qualification that would be applicable for CSWs working in both the schools and further education sectors. Research suggested that this was possible. Even TDA agreed that the proposal should be possible. However, a visit to TDA's offices in Manchester on 25 September 2009 to discuss the proposal proved to be quite disappointing. TDA agreed with the proposal and even suggested that some of their units could be appropriate to include in a qualification structure which would encompass those CSWs working in both sectors.

Unfortunately the proposal was not straightforward. TDA reluctantly announced that they were not in a position, at that time, to work on this development and suggested that such a proposal may be possible in a couple of years. Understandably this was very disappointing but, as the project had very tight deadlines to adhere to, it was impossible to wait for two years to work with TDA. It is worth noting that at the time of writing, more than two years after that initial meeting, TDA's response is still the same whenever the suggestion of developing a qualification for schools based CSWs is raised. TDA state that, regrettably, they have neither the funding nor the time to devote to the proposal at present. The decision therefore was reluctantly made to concentrate on developing a qualification solely with LLUK and thereby concentrate on a qualification for CSWs working in the FE sector.

Competitors

At that time, there was also reluctance for people to accept that Signature should be the awarding body of the new qualification for CSWs. Since 1992 Edexcel had awarded the only nationally recognised CSW qualification, admittedly in a variety of guises, whilst Signature had always concentrated on qualifications involving Deafness, Communication and British Sign Language (BSL). Signature did consider jointly awarding the qualification with Edexcel. A meeting was held at Edexcel's offices in London on 14 September 2009 to discuss this proposal. Unfortunately it was explained that the CSW qualification had attracted so few candidates in latter years and was offered by so few centres that Edexcel had decided, from a purely business point of view, that they would no longer include it in their portfolio. If there was a demand to train CSWs to a nationally recognised qualification, Signature as an awarding body, would have no competitors. Any resistance soon disappeared once this was made clear.

Signature then had the task of being given permission to operate in the education sector, because up until that point, all their work had been in the language sector. After more reports and discussions, permission was granted. Another obstacle had been removed and Signature were able to broaden their qualification portfolio.

National Occupational Standards

In addition to trying to develop a specialist pathway for CSWs using the LLUK model, National Occupational Standards (NOS) for CSWs needed to be developed. It was vital that NOS be developed if CSWs were to achieve professional recognition. The overall aim was to develop a new qualification and to raise the status of CSWs in an attempt to have the workforce recognised as the true professionals that they have always been. In order to achieve professional status, the qualification needed national recognition, to achieve full accreditation, to appear on the national Learning Aims Database, and be supported by NOS. LLUK had already developed NOS for learning support practitioners in 2008. The task was now to develop an Application Guide which would define the Application of the National Occupational Standards for Learning Support Staff who provide Communication Support.

LLUK were leading on the development of the NOS Application Guide for CSWs. This was something that could not be done alone—help was needed. The expertise that the committees of NATED and ACSW shared between them proved to be invaluable. A couple of meetings were arranged between Maria, Paul Hambley of LLUK and committee members of NATED and ACSW, the first one being held on

9 November 2009 in Stafford. By this time both NATED and ACSW were willing to assist with the development. Once again there were numerous reports to be written and very tight deadlines to meet. Amazingly, the NOS Application Guide was developed, on time, to the satisfaction of LLUK. At this point it is worth noting the remarkable efforts of all who were involved in the process. In particular, two people, Andy Owen and Jill Bussien took on the responsibility of developing the Standard C 'Elements relating to CSWs' within the Application Guide despite a very tight deadline. Incredibly it was some considerable time later, in March 2011, when the NOS Application Guide was finally approved and published by LLUK. However, it now exists – another significant achievement. The full Application Guide can be found on Signature's website, and further information on the NOS is included in Chapter 10.

Supporting Bilingual Access

Considerable discussion was had with the NATED committee and others on the content of the 'additional' units required to create the CSW pathway. Maria lost count of the number of proposed structures which were presented and discounted for one reason or another. Eventually the structure of the new CSW qualification was finally agreed. Acknowledgement is made to Jill Newlands who developed the unit entitled 'Supporting Bilingual Access.' This unit concentrates on voice-over skills and gives candidates strategies to use to overcome problems that may arise. This is a vital component of the new qualification, which was sadly missing from previous CSW training.

On 30 June 2010, news was received that Signature had achieved accreditation for the new CSW qualification. Despite all the barriers, the mission had been accomplished.

It is fair to say that most people, as customers of Signature, who use the organisation either as a student, whilst studying BSL (British Sign Language) or as a customer whilst working at colleges and arranging examinations for students, have no idea how such an organisation works. Almost everyone, at some point or another, has complained about how long people must wait to receive results of examinations, how much notice needs to be given to arrange examinations etc. Not surprisingly, working on the inside, one gets a very different perspective and a greater understanding of how such an organisation operates. Signature is an awarding body and develops qualifications. It has to adhere to very strict regulations and guidelines issued by government controlled organisations including OfQual (Office of Qualifications and Examinations Regulation) and JCQ (Joint Council for Qualifications), which appear to change as frequently as the weather. Signature is a relatively small organisation which is a constant hive of activity. It relies on external examiners and assessors to carry out most of the work involving the actual assessing/examining of candidates. When one therefore spends some time inside the organisation, one cannot fail to be full of admiration for all that they manage to achieve, to a very high professional standard. Whilst gaining an understanding of how a relatively small organisation like Signature works under such constant pressure, it was very frustrating to experience the extensive delays when trying to work with other organisations including LLUK and TDA. When working on a project, there are constant deadlines that must be met. Sometimes it was not possible to meet certain deadlines, not because work had not been done, but often because of delays, waiting for responses from external organisations. Very frustrating, but nothing that anyone could physically do to hurry things along.

Between July 2010 and the end of the I Sign project in March 2011, time was spent developing teaching materials and teacher support packs for centres who were granted Centre Approval to offer the CSW qualification. Visits were made to a number of colleges who had expressed an interest in offering the CSW course and presentations were given. Once accreditation had been achieved, the task was to encourage centres to offer the course to meet the demand.

Maria was invited to speak at the joint NATED/ACSW conferences in 2010 and 2011 to give upates of the development of the new qualification for CSWs. These presentations raised a great deal of interest in the development, and heated question and answer sessions followed. Following the 2010 conference in Greenwich, Maria became a co-opted committee member of NATED in September that year.

First Pilot Centre

City College Coventry became the first centre to pilot the new qualification. Teaching commenced in October 2010 and candidates submitted their portfolios of evidence in July 2011. All candidates were successful and the work produced was of a very high standard. The two main lecturers on the course, Emma Green and Jane Blundell had been involved in the development of teaching materials and course content with Maria and were very happy to be training the first group of newly qualified CSWs. Sadly, ERADE were unable to continue with their intention to pilot the CSW course alongside City College Coventry, due to internal restructuring and the loss of key members of staff. However, Jane Godwin was fully involved throughout the development process and met frequently with Emma Green, Jane Blundell and Maria, so her contribution is also acknowledged.

In summary, there is now a nationally recognised qualification, and National Occupational Standards for CSWs. There (hopefully) will soon be a registration category for CSWs on the NRCPD (The National Register of Communication Professionals working with Deaf People). This should enable CSWs to be recognised as professionals in their own right. As such, CSWs should always strive to improve themselves and update their skills. Even though so much has been achieved, there is much to do. The next phase is to aim to ensure that all CSWs receive appropriate training and ongoing support. Unfortunately the new developments have come at a time of increasing funding cuts under the current coalition government, quite the reverse of the funding situation during the early days of CSW training in the late 1980s. One can only hope that this issue can be resolved soon and that CSWs will continue to be trained and recognised appropriately for what they do.

Finally, let us never forget that CSWs work to aid access to the world of education for all Deaf students, whatever the age, ability, background or level of hearing loss. Without them, there would be no need for CSWs. We need to continue to work together to improve the service that we offer and to fight for appropriate funding and support.

The struggle continues.

13
The First Signature CSW Pilot Course

A s part of the I-Sign Project, the intention was always to pilot the new Signature qualification for Communication Support Workers (CSWs) in two distinct geographical areas. The areas identified in the project were the North West and the South West of England. It was in these two areas that other strands of the project were to be piloted.

Exeter Royal Academy of Deaf Education (ERADE) quickly volunteered themselves as the South West pilot centre. Contact was soon made with Jane Godwin, CSW manager at ERADE and a very good working relationship between Jane and Maria Bailey (Signature's I-Sign Project Officer) soon developed. ERADE have a very long history of training CSWs and for a number of years had used an Open College Network (OCN) qualification. However the benefits of delivering a nationally recognised qualification to their staff were soon identified and

ERADE were keen to be among the first centres to pilot the new course.

The search for the second pilot centre, ideally situated in the North West was not so straightforward. After many unsuccessful attempts to identify an appropriate centre in this area, City College Coventry made contact with Maria Bailey and expressed an interest in being involved in the project. Negotiations to identify City College Coventry as the second pilot centre soon began. It was considered that, due to their experience of delivering CSWs training, they would be an appropriate centre to work with. Another important factor was that Coventry was considered to be sufficiently geographically remote from Exeter to make the decision justifiable.

Developmental Meetings

Several developmental meetings were held between Maria Bailey, Jane Godwin of ERADE and Emma Green and Jane Blundell of City College Coventry between June 2009 and July 2010. During this time, many teaching resources were developed including Teacher Support Guides for each of the units in the Signature CSW qualification. Plans were made for both centres to start recruiting candidates and to, hopefully, start delivering the training in September 2010.

Unfortunately, due to unforeseen circumstances, ERADE were not able to continue with their plans to pilot the training and, reluctantly, had to withdraw their involvement in the summer of 2010.

City College Coventry have a long history of training CSWs. They were one of the first colleges in the country to offer CSW training, following the very first MSC (Manpower Services Commission) funded course in 1986/7 at Bournville College, Birmingham and Birmingham Institute for the Deaf (BID), led by Warren Nickerson. In 1987, at the start of the second year of the three year MSC project, Warren Nickerson moved to Coventry to set up ECSTRA (Education, Communication, Support, Training, Retraining and Advice for Deaf Adults) and continued delivering the CSW training there. Since 1992, the Edexcel CSW training was offered.The demand for CSW training continued and a course was usually offered every two years. Occasionally there were two separate intakes in one year to meet the demand. The training was always held one day per week over a full academic year.

As a lecturer at City College Coventry, Emma Green started delivering CSW training in about 2000. Before then, other tutors were involved. CSW training has always been delivered by a team of different people. City College Coventry have always employed four tutors for deaf students in SASU (Student Access Support Unit, formerly known as ECSTRA). One was a Teacher of the Deaf (ToD), then there were three others, including Emma, Nicki Richards (who has a partial hearing loss) and Paul Tansell, who is Deaf. They all taught different units on the Edexcel course and would bring in outside speakers too. Paul was lead tutor on the CSW course. Nicki and Jo (ToD) taught the majority of it. Then, as time went on Emma taught more and more. Emma can't remember exactly how she became involved in teaching the CSW course, perhaps someone was off sick, she mused, but she was invited to be involved and carried on from there.

City College Coventry started to deliver the first pilot of the new Signature Level 3 Certificate in Learning Support (Communication Support Workers) in October 2010. Unfortunately, despite a great deal of initial interest and numerous enquiries, the number of candidates enrolled on the course was low, but sufficient to enable the course to proceed. Lack of financial support by employers was given as one of the reasons why applicants were unable to undertake the training on offer. The interest in the training remains high but sadly, due partly to the current economic situation and uncertainty over employment, people are being understandably extra cautious and are not willing to commit to additional financial outlays, despite the desire to undertake training to enhance their career prospects. Despite this, the candidates at City College were all keen and, during an informal visit to the college in 2011, informed Maria Bailey that they had all enjoyed the training and felt that they had learnt a great deal from it.

A Broader and More Flexible CSW Course

When asked what her opinion was of the new Signature CSW course, after being one of the first tutors to deliver the new training, Emma replied that she thinks it is a far broader course now. It's far more appropriate and far more flexible. It allows more opportunities in a broader field. Emma considers this to be what is needed nowadays. The previous Edexcel course had, in Emma's opinion, very little content about working in other types of education. The Signature course covers the whole spectrum. Emma thinks the new CSW course will appeal to more people now.

Asked about whether she had enjoyed being involved in piloting the new course, Emma replied 'Yes, it's been an adventure, hasn't it? The students all did well and have gone on to find employment, some working as CSWs, one working freelance and one doing voluntary work in the community.' This was a positive response and very good to hear. Emma Green and Jane Blundell should be very proud of being the main tutors of the very first new style CSW course. They will both go down in CSW history.

The initial pilot of the Signature Level 3 Certificate in Learning Support (Communication Support Workers) ended in July 2011. All candidates submitted portfolios which were internally assessed and externally moderated. All work submitted was of a very high standard. All candidates were successful and have now achieved the Signature certificate.

Another important chapter in the history of CSWs.

14
The Discrete Role of the CSW

The acronym CSW (communication support worker) is well known, but the role may not be universally understood. Indeed, many CSWs are unsure of what their role entails, for reasons discussed later in this chapter, and partly because employers are not sure, and regard the acronym as a general umbrella term to apply to all their staff working with Deaf learners. It is therefore important to be able to identify the role, so this chapter addresses that issue. It is also important to identify a discrete CSW role because there are other discrete roles working with Deaf people, such as interpreter, lipspeaker, manual and electronic notetaker etc., each having a category within the National Registers for Communication Professionals working with Deaf and Deafblind People (NRCPD).

Much of this chapter is gleaned from a proposal for opening a category for CSWs in the NRCPD. This proposal was formally presented to the NRCPD on the 15th of February 2012. ACSW took the lead in producing it, with the agreement of NATED, and it was supported by the DESF (Deaf Education Support Forum) at that time comprising representatives of ACSW, Action on Hearing Loss (formerly RNID), the Association of Notetaking Professionals (ANP), the Association of Sign Language Interpreters (ASLI), the British Association of Teachers of the Deaf (BATOD), the Consortium of Higher Education Support Services with Deaf Students (CHESS), Mary Hare Training, NATED, and Signature. The proposal therefore represented a meeting of minds of the main stakeholder organisations involved in the education of Deaf students of all ages. Members of the DESF made several amendments to the proposal prior to its submission, so it constituted a document that was considered and relevant.

What the CSWs Role is Not

An explanation of the discrete role of the CSW may benefit from a description of what the CSW role is not, because we will then begin to narrow down the field to address what the role actually is. There are several mistaken views of the role of the CSW and it would be useful to consider these. Three are briefly discussed here.

1. The 'CSWs Have Too Many Roles' View

The view that the role of CSW is difficult to identify because it has many parts, is held by many people. Many believe that it is impossible to become qualified and proficient in all parts and use the figure of speech: 'Jack of all trades, master of none' to describe a person who is competent in many skills, but not necessarily outstanding in any particular one. Frank Harrington expounded this view in his document, 'The Rise,

Fall and Re-invention of the Communicator: re-defining roles and responsibilities in educational interpreting' (2001). Harrington says:

> I am not convinced that the roles carried out by CSWs can appropriately remain the responsibility of one individual, or that the training available to them at present adequately prepares them for all of the tasks they undertake.

It could be that this view has been a sticking-point for CSWs becoming registered because those who hold this view, and/or those who have been influenced by this view, find it difficult to pin down just what the CSW role is. It means that other roles have been assigned to the CSW, such as notetaker, lipspeaker or interpreter, in an attempt to understand or identify just what the role is. But this intellectual re-assigning of roles has served to perpetuate the confusion and has laid CSWs open to criticism that they are not qualified to undertake the roles that have been re-assigned to them. This view may lie behind the belief that there should be a multi-layered CSW qualification, and by extension, a multi-level registration category based on BSL levels, which is a mistaken view.

It is true that in the search for developing personal skills, many CSWs have been able to achieve qualifications in other areas, such as notetaking, qualified teacher status, plus a range of other roles not intrinsic but complementary to the CSW role. Those qualifications have not served to change the role – rather they have enhanced it. As Peter Llewellyn-Jones has commented in his report in chapter 6, he has 'no argument at all with the breadth of role that the CSW has' because he argues that 'any competent interpreter needs that breadth of role also'. It is important therefore, that the discrete role of the CSW should not be dependent upon nor conflict with the skills or qualifications assigned to the roles of other professionals working with Deaf or Deafblind people, but rather, it

278 History of Communication Support Workers

should depend upon the National Occupation Standards for CSWs, expanded in the Standards Application Guide, in much the same way that the discrete interpreter role depends on the National Occupational Standards in Interpreting (CILT 2006).

2. The 'CSWs Are Not Teachers' View

This view is that CSWs should not be performing a teaching function without appropriate qualifications, which most do not have. This view states that any literacy work must be undertaken by a Teacher of the Deaf, Support Tutor or similar specialist. Some provisions propose this model, that CSWs simply go into the classroom to provide access to the curriculum, usually through BSL, then report back to the ToD, who meets with the learner from time to time to work on literacy. These provisions view CSWs as 'interpreters-in-waiting', and those CSWs who pass through and become qualified interpreters may not fully grasp the value and breadth of the CSW role.

Other provisions however, hold the view that the CSW is at the 'chalkface' in the classroom, therefore in a much better position to make immediate judgements without delay and make full use of the concepts and skills gained from CSW courses. At the direction of the ToD (who may well be peripatetic and whose time is limited) the CSW performs aspects of literary support, documents events, feeds back and discusses issues with the ToD, who works with the CSW and others in the team to achieve educational outcomes. This view is held by at least one Head of Service, who in chapter 9 says of his team:

> Staff therefore need to take those students from where they currently are and move them onto the next appropriate emotional and cognitive phase. I see my team of CSWs being directly involved in that process.

The 'CSWs are not teachers' belief is instrumental in promoting a view of the CSW role as a stepping-stone to interpreter status, because it limits the CSW role to an interpreting function, of necessity requiring constant improvement, and marginalises many facets of the CSW role as identified in the National Occupation Standards for CSWs, expanded in the Standards Application Guide. It denies oral Deaf learners the opportunity to make use of qualified CSWs who have the appropriate skills to steer them through the educational pathway, and misleads those who eventually become interpreters into thinking they performed the proper role of CSW.

3. The 'CSWs Should Not Interpret' View

This view is that CSWs should not be performing an interpreting function without interpreting qualifications, which most do not have. This view states that most CSWs have inadequate BSL skills, let alone those required for interpreting. CSWs are perceived as less qualified and less skilled people, who therefore should not be supporting Deaf students.

This is both a developmental and a domain-specific issue. It is a developmental issue because a growing number of CSWs hold BSL/English interpreting qualifications. One example of this is a snapshot of the Royal Greenwich Sensory Service in London. From a team of twenty CSWs, five are qualified interpreters, two completed interpreting training leading to trainee status at the end of the 2011-12 academic year, and one is studying for an MA in interpreting. It is a domain-specific issue because individual CSWs should be assigned to domains that match their skill-set. That is, to match the specific skills of each CSW to specific age groups of learners, subjects, or the communication/personal needs of individual learners.

The claim that the main role of the CSW is to interpret between BSL and English requires constant appraisal because the communication requirements of Deaf students are constantly shifting. In 2011, the Consortium for Research into Deaf Education (CRIDE) conducted a UK-wide survey on educational staffing and service provision for Deaf children in the 2010/11 financial year. The report states that there are at least 34,927 Deaf children in England, but only 9% use sign language to some extent to communicate. These findings do not contain data for those who no longer have an educational statement, having progressed to further education, but the findings do show that the preferred communication method used by a majority of Deaf learners is not BSL. Therefore, many CSWs work with Deaf students who do not sign, and those who prefer to lip read requiring the occasional sign or note to keep them on track, and some prefer to have notes only. An increasing number are cochlear implant users who require speech, Sign Supported English, or simply some curriculum support with their written work. These requirements have few or no features of interpreting.

The 'CSWs are not interpreters' view is instrumental in promoting a view of the CSW role as a stepping-stone to interpreter status (Signature 2009). This view also propounds the suspicion that CSWs are not concerned about professional development. The mistake however, lies in two misconceptions: 1. that all CSWs want to be interpreters, 2. that interpreting is what CSWs mainly do. It is important therefore, that the discrete role of the CSW should not be founded on interpreting skills or interpreting qualifications, but rather, it should be founded upon the National Occupation Standards, expanded in the Standards Application Guide. Therefore, we must now turn to these documents.

National Occupational Standards

The discrete role of the CSW must spring from and mirror the Occupational Standards of the role itself. This is especially important within a register such as the NRCPD (National Registers of Communication Professionals working with Deaf and Deafblind People) where roles may overlap. Overlapping takes place because all the roles have a mutual occupation, of 'Communication Professionals'. Also, all the roles operate within the remit of communication with Deaf and Deafblind people. As has been stated, it is important that the discrete role of the CSW should not be founded upon the skills or qualifications assigned to the roles of other categories in the NRCPD, but rather, the role should depend upon the National Occupational Standards and the Application Guide for CSWs.

Standards Application Guide

The National Occupational Standards Application Guide (NOSAG) is a guidance document that applies the National Occupational Standards for learning support practitioners to the role of the CSW. An application guidance document like this provides more detail for occupation standards and can be written for any suite of standards and for a particular context such as offender learning, for a particular subject such as literacy and numeracy or for a particular group of people such as CSWs working with Deaf learners.

This NOSAG for CSWs was produced by Signature in association with NATED, ACSW and Lifelong Learning UK, in response to the Government-funded I-Sign Project. One of the strands within the project was to develop a qualification for CSWs supporting Deaf students in education. That qualification sprang from the NOSAG, which means that it was a three-step process: The National Occupation Standards, the Application Guide, and the Qualification. It was therefore a robust and thorough consultative process that charts and details the discrete role of the CSW. There should therefore be no confusion as to the role of the CSW.

What Quality of Person is a CSW?

Any discussion of a discrete CSW role that springs from Occupational Standards and Application Guides will be the bare bones, so we must flesh-out the role and discuss what sort of person takes on the CSW role. We must also look at the CSW Code of Practice, held by NATED, and finally, consider those CSWs who prefer to work outside the the educational domain.

The Stability of the CSW

A watchword in education is 'continuity', which is an issue when students go through transitions between primary and secondary, and between secondary and tertiary settings. It is an issue when parents are posted regularly to different geographical locations (armed forces personnel), or when children leave home to attend boarding school. Continuity is also an issue when a teacher leaves and another joins during a course. As a measure to promote continuity, a teacher's typical/standard contract of employment states that, should they wish to leave their institution/position or end their contract, one term's notice must be given. Many CSWs have a similar contract, and like teachers, are not able to take leave of work during term time except for illness or some other serious event, and certainly not for a holiday.

Working in education therefore requires a commitment that is accepted as integral to the ethos of education. The majority of CSWs accept that commitment as part of the role. Crucially, this has an impact on assessment. In an examination situation, the CSW often performs the function of an Oral Language Modifier, which is an access provision that includes Deaf candidates, regulated by the Joint Council for Qualifications (JCQ). Their regulations (2011-12) state:

> 2.11.3 The provision of an Oral Language Modifier should reflect the candidate's normal way of working within the centre and should be appropriate to the needs of the candidate.
>
> The candidate should be familiar with the Oral Language Modifier. Where this is not the case, the candidate must have the opportunity to familiarise him/herself with the Oral Language Modifier using a trial presentation. The candidate must be comfortable with the method of communication.

The CSW who has been working with a Deaf learner through a course will know the content, structure and vocabulary of the course and will be in a better position to work with the learner when he or she becomes a candidate in an examination. Moreover, the CSW will be working toward this as the course proceeds, identifying subject-specific vocabulary, training the learner to identify the English vocabulary independently (not just the BSL) and working with the learner to expect a different sort of support in the examination room. The CSW will also work with subject staff to have in place appropriate provisions such as extra time in mock examinations, so that the learner can pace him or herself and be aware of the different convention of support so that there are no surprises in the examination room. A freelance interpreter (or indeed CSW) used for a one-off booking to interpret for a Deaf candidate in an examination is therefore inappropriate.

The Outlook of the CSW

It has been argued (see chapter 9) that all adults working in a classroom situation should have the outlook; 'educator'. For those who work in education; teacher, teaching assistant, CSW or interpreter, the outlook of 'educator' is shared by the whole team. The role of teacher is a specialism that may not shared by the CSW (except in the case of the CSW also holding a teaching qualification) but the CSW supports the aim of the teacher, which is to educate. This is supported by at least one head of service, who in chapter 9, pondered whether CSWs should be described as educators or perhaps actually, they are teachers, albeit on the unqualified teacher's pay scale. For many interpreters however, the outlook often remains, 'interpreter'. This is reinforced by the Association of Sign Language Interpreters (ASLI) document: 'Guidelines for interpreters working in educational settings', which has the following headings: Professional Conduct, Complete and effective communication, Impartiality, Confidentiality and Competence. The document is a good resource for an individual whose aim is to provide good quality interpreting, because these headings are important and could be applicable to any domain. The document does not however address the issue of being included in the collective educational team, and what impact that inclusion has on an individual's outlook. Those who perform the role of CSW require an outlook that addresses other important educational issues, such as those which are taught within the Signature CSW training course and other similar training courses. But that is not all – because the outlook of the CSW is to promote education, it follows that it is also instrumental, together with the role of teacher (Brooks 2008, and Segal 1988) in fostering resilience and self-esteem in Deaf children and young people. The role not only aims to provide access to curriculii, but aims to develop the individual Deaf learner holistically.

Education is arguably one of the most difficult of domains, and often demands a multitude of duties that a CSW is accustomed to performing: cleaning juvenile clients' hearing aids, testing and changing batteries, rearranging a room to become acoustically appropriate, building long-term reciprocal relationships with teaching staff and students, modifying teaching resources to match appropriate levels of English for Deaf students, promoting Deaf awareness by organising events for staff and students, being flexible and willing to use SSE (Sign Supported English), BSL (British Sign Language), notetaking or whatever is required for understanding to take place. These are accepted functions and the personal attitude of CSWs reflect the need for these functions to be performed.

The CSW Code of Practice

The CSW Code of Practice (2007) is held by NATED, influential when the original CSW course was coming into being, and remaining so. The Code was updated in 2007 when ACSW was a young association, indeed some of the new ACSW committee attended the national consultation meetings. ACSW endorse and support the Code of Practice, which is going through the updating process again as this volume is being written. Updating the Code involves input from stakeholders and dovetailing with other progressions such as the National Occupation Standards, Application Guide and CSW course developments.

Extracts from the Code:

The role of the CSW is:
a. To enable equal access for Deaf learners to information in the curriculum and college environment, according to the assessed needs of the Deaf learner.
b. To encourage the development of the individual Deaf learner within educational, social, linguistic and cultural contexts, providing support which is empowering

through the development of a range of appropriate strategies.

c. To consider the needs of the Deaf learner within the context of their peer group, and to provide appropriate communication strategies, from a range of skills, helping to facilitate successful integration of the group.

d. To provide access to a range of learning materials using appropriate communication methods to match the needs of the individual Deaf learner.

e. To respond to all communication requirements that may arise in the learning environment, and to implement, review and adapt strategies as necessary.

f. To enable and empower learners to discuss their own learning requirements with teaching staff.

g. To provide Deaf awareness, advice and guidance for teaching staff and/or peer group and to involve the Deaf learners whenever possible. This may be ongoing.

h. To facilitate access to wider college services, e.g. counselling, financial support, library and learning resources etc.

i. To, wherever possible, work collaboratively in a team which assesses and delivers and reviews the Deaf learner's individual support needs.

j. To enable Deaf learners to make independent choices and learn from their own experiences.

k. To keep accurate records of work and perform support-related administration as required, e.g. for purposes of management, inspection and audit.

As NATED is an association founded and working in education, it is natural, therefore that a) they should hold the Code of Practice, and b) the Code of Practice places CSWs in education.

The CSW Working Outside Education

Technically, a 'qualified CSW' is a person who is qualified to work in education. All the past manifestations of CSW qualifications were focused on CSWs working in education, and the present Signature qualification is no exception. This means that when someone is described as a 'qualified CSW', that person has been trained to perform the role within education. However, a great deal of the theory taught on those courses is applicable for domains outside education, and CSWs who find themselves in a 'work' environment can draw on those theories. This benefits aspiring interpreters who pass through CSW training, because they imbibe an explicit understanding of the educational development, cognition and language of Deaf people, and gain an understanding of collaboration and the need to consistently improve competence. Indeed, much of the CSW course content would benefit inclusion into interpreter training.

There is no qualification for CSWs who wish to work outside education. There will always be problems providing courses for niche candidate groups because of costing, availability of trainers and centres to run such courses. Having an available CSW qualification founded in education (where the vast majority of CSWs work) has been a battle, as this book explains (see chapter 10). A training course for CSWs who prefer to work outside education may therefore remain an aspiration unless a champion comes forward. ACSW recognises that some of their members work outside the educational domain and supports them. However, the association recommends that any such CSW should undertake an available CSW qualification regardless of domain, have a current Criminal Records Bureau check and Professional Indemnity insurance, and be able to consider personal competences.

15
Supporting Organisations

This section gives an insight into the background of some of the organisations considered to have played a key part in the history of communication support workers (CSWs).

NATED

The National Association for Tertiary Education for the Deaf.

The origins of NATED

In 1976 a small group of Teachers of the Deaf working as individuals in colleges, were invited by Peter Greenwood to meet in Bradford to share experiences and professional support. They started by collating examination arrangements for Deaf students. The group decided to hold a bigger, regional meeting to include more people and this took place in Sheffield in 1977. It led to a national meeting and the National Study Group in Further Education for the Hearing Impaired was established, with Joyce Sutton as the first Chair. The group became NATED in 1984, and founder members, besides Peter Greenwood and Joyce Sutton, included Mike Hanson, Joe Pearce and John Hatton. Sadly Peter Greenwood died in the Bradford City Football Stadium fire in 1985, and Joe Pearce died at the grand old age of 90.

This group was responsible for all the early work with examination boards in negotiating examination arrangements. They promoted the need for clear communication and language modification and developed the 'Language of Examinations' booklet.

The aims of NATED

- Promote good practice and quality support services for Deaf learners in tertiary education
- Provide training and networking opportunities, and advice and guidance for professionals working with Deaf learners
- Work with other agencies and professional bodies to ensure that their policies and procedures promote fair assessment and opportunities for all Deaf learners
- Produce publications to encourage good practice, such as appropriate assessment procedures, support provision, updating of policies and highlighting current topics of concern.
- Assist the development of effective transition into and beyond further education.
- Involvement in developing training courses and resources for professionals working with Deaf learners in tertiary education across the UK.

NATED achievements

Over the years NATED has worked:

- To raise awareness about Deafness, developing information packs for lecturers

- To support Deaf students entering further education (FE) – there was a pack for them too
- To establish communication support workers, originally for YTS (Youth Training Scheme) trainees
- To develop materials for the assessment for support needs
- To provide information and networking opportunities for people interested in the further and higher education of Deaf students
- To contribute to government consultations advising administrations of the implications for supporting Deaf learners
- To liaise with groups such as BATOD (British Association of Teachers of the Deaf), SKILL (National Bureau for Students with Disabilities), RNID (Royal National Institute for Deaf People), BDA (British Deaf Association), NDCS (National Deaf Children's Society), ASLI (Association of Sign Language Interpreters) to promote opportunities and facilitate access to FE and HE (Higher Education) for Deaf learners
- To work with CACDP (Council for the Advancement of Communication with Deaf People - now Signature) and Edexcel in the development of professional qualifications.

Thirty eight years has seen a significant change in the culture of FE with regard to students with disabilities or learning difficulties.

Government initiatives, informed by groups like NATED, have led to policies on inclusive learning and widening participation, with funding arrangements which can accommodate adjustments for Deaf and hard of hearing learners. Where there is funding, there is accountability, demand for quality and continuous improvement of service. Yet we still need to raise awareness, support colleagues as well as learners, advise administrations and partners, develop qualifications and re-invent arrangements which have toppled as a result of change or shifting legislation. Status Quo requires maintenance!

Adapted from the NATED website: http://www.nated.org

ACSW

The Association of Communication Support Workers.

ACSW, constituted in 2006, supports communication support workers (CSWs) and those who use their services. CSWs work with Deaf learners of all ages, levels and ability using the individual's preferred method of communication to enable access in educational settings. ACSW supports some CSWs who are employed in roles outside of education but the current qualifications focus on education only.

ACSW is a national association that aims to support and represent the interests and views of CSWs and their Deaf users. The Association seeks to encourage good practice in communication support and to improve the training standards and opportunities for current and future CSWs.

The Association aims to provide a network for CSWs, prospective CSWs and Deaf users to exchange information, views and ideas. The Association also provides a platform for change, and committee members are elected to promote the aims of the organisation and its members.

Why do CSWs need an Association?

ACSW was set up to promote and encourage good practice amongst CSWs and to gain recognition of the work undertaken by thousands of people in the UK. The Association works with other organisations to improve training, recognition and to tackle policies. Members of ACSW are facilitating the progression of CSWs to achieve professional status in the future.

The role of the CSW is hotly debated but ACSW believes that CSWs play an important role in a learner's education. CSWs use a variety of direct and indirect support strategies dependent on the needs of individual learners. ACSW actively encourages anyone interested in becoming a CSW to obtain the Signature Level 3 Certificate in Learning Support (Communication Support Worker) qualification. It also promotes continuous professional development and offers some informal training opportunities for members as well as non-members. Training held by various organisations is often advertised on the ACSW forum under the Jobs and Opportunities section.

Members of the ACSW committee are able to represent CSWs at a national consultative level and have been involved in amending regulations for the benefit of CSWs nationally and the Deaf learners they work with.

Further information can be found on the ACSW website: http://www.acsw.org.uk

DESF

Deaf Education Support Forum.

This forum commenced in June 2009. The DESF initially comprised representatives of ACSW, ASLI (Association of Sign Language Interpreters), BATOD (British Association of Teachers of the Deaf), NATED and Signature, for the sharing of information, the pooling of expertise and the discussion of issues related to the education of Deaf students of all ages. The first formal meeting took place on 22 June 2009 at the RNID (Royal National Institute for Deaf People) headquarters in Central London. The group later expanded further and welcomed representatives of Mary Hare Training, the Consortium of Higher Education Support Services (CHESS), the Association of Notetaking Professionals (ANP) and the RNID itself (thus securing the venue for the meetings). By nature of the significance of the collective members, it quickly commanded a reputation. Since then, meetings have been held once every academic term.

The first challenge was to identify a national snapshot of titles, training and qualifications of staff working in Deaf education. Andy Owen offered to requisition and amend a questionnaire devised by Vicky Nunn and used in a limited capacity by ACSW. This became the DESF Survey that eventually was published at the end of 2010. The findings were to be fascinating and confirmed what was known anecdotally. The DESF Survey is planned to be produced every two years.

SIGNATURE

History of Signature

In 1976, the British Deaf Association submitted an application for the funding of a Communication Skills Project to the Department of Health and Social Security. The project was a response to the Association's concern that sign language skills were declining at a time when Deaf people were becoming aware of the educational, economic and social opportunities available and the need for sign language interpreting.

The three-year Communication Skills Project was approved and received £133,000 which, at the time, was one of the largest grants in support of Deaf people. Towards the end of this project there was a concern that the progress made would be halted or lost unless there was an organisation capable of continuing the work.

CACDP

As a result, the Council for the Advancement of Communication with Deaf People (CACDP) was formed in December 1980 and became an independent organisation in 1982. Because of the Communication Skills Project much of CACDP's early work was focused on sign language and sign language interpreting and a register of communication professionals was established. At first, only BSL/English interpreters were able to register but this was later expanded to include speech to text reporters, lipspeakers, notetakers, and Deafblind interpreters (manual).

Over a thirty year history, a portfolio of qualifications was developed in communication skills. These qualifications have gained widespread recognition and have given approximately 300,000 people the opportunity to communicate directly with Deaf and Deafblind people.

First Accredited Qualifications

The NQF (National Qualification Framework) was set up in 2000 so CACDP were able to launch their first accredited qualifications from 1 October 2001. These included Level 1 Certificate in BSL and ISL, Level 1 Certificate in Deaf Awareness and Level 1 Certificate in Communication Tactics with Deaf People. Qualifications are nationally recognised and accredited by Ofqual (The Office of the Qualifications and Examinations Regulator) and some are also on the Scottish Credit and Qualifications Framework (SCQF). CACDP have overcome many obstacles to become a recognised professional registration body and one of the top awarding bodies in the UK.

Becoming Signature

Success drove CACDP to take stock and give a greater focus towards a vision of a society in which Deaf people have full access. The commitment to share knowledge and recognise skills in the languages and communication methods used by Deaf and Deafblind people led CACDP to become Signature in January 2009.

Adapted from the Signature website: http://www.signature. org.uk/page.php?content=63

16
Summary

The twenty five years that have passed since the first qualified communication support workers (CSWs) entered the
workforce in 1987 have seen changes beyond imagination.
Memorable events in 1987 include: work commencing on the
Channel Tunnel connecting England and France, disposable
contact lenses becoming available for commercial distribution,
Clive Sinclair launching the Z88 Portable Computer, weighing
less than 2lbs (less than one kilogram).

In 1987 orange, apple and blackberry were simply fruit.
The very idea of advances in technology, for example Skype,
which would enable people to have a face-to-face conversation using a small computer would have been classed as pure
science fiction. Digital hearing aids, cochlear implants, email,
social networking including facebook and twitter, texting and
iPhones were for the future. These are just a few of the changes

in technology that have taken place over the last twenty five years. What a difference they have made to all our lives and how we communicate.

In 1987 the term British Sign Language was not used. Sign language interpreting was a new profession which had been introduced in the 1980s. Simpson (2004) remarks that 'In 1981 there were very few occasions when sign language inter- preters were used in meetings attended by the general public. Deaf people were not expected to be there...' (Simpson, 2007, p51). Simpson also comments that 'Prior to the 1970s few, very few, Deaf people entered further or higher education. It was not expected they would... By the 1980s, increasing numbers of Deaf students of all abilities were seeking to enter further, (and, to a much lesser extent, higher) education (Simpson, 2007, p173). From these examples alone, it is possible to see the amount of progress that has been made towards opening access for Deaf people during the past twenty five years.

Green and Nickerson, in the final chapter of their 1992 book, mentioned the expectation that 1993 would bring, follow- ing the introduction of the Further and Higher Education Act 1992. It was expected that a fundamental change to the whole structure and funding of further education would be witnessed (Green and Nickerson, 1992, p227). It therefore seemed fitting to look briefly at the changes in legislation during the inter- vening years and acknowledge the effect on the changes in attitudes and general awareness towards Deafness and other disabilities they have brought in the final chapter of this book.

Developments in Legislation

The Disability Discrimination Act (DDA) 1995 had a profound effect on the way that society treated disabled people. The DDA made it unlawful for disabled people to be treated 'less favourably' than non-disabled people. 'Reasonable adjustments' had to be made in order for disabled people to gain full access to various sectors of society including employment, access to goods and services and transport. The DDA was amended over the years to include protection from discrimination in other areas.

2001 saw the introduction of the Special Educational Needs and Discrimination Act (SENDA) which gave protection against discrimination in schools and other educational establishments under new provisions in Part 4 of the DDA.

The Disability Rights Commission Act 1999 replaced the National Disability Council with the Disability Rights Commission (DRC).

The Equality Act 2006 transferred the role of the DRC to the Equality and Human Rights Commission (Legislation.gov [online, n.d.]).

Each piece of legislation introduced new rights for disabled people and society needed to adjust to prevent discrimination and remove many of the barriers that disabled people had always faced.

CSWs Arrived on the Scene

Qualified CSWs entered the workforce in 1987 and this book has attempted to illustrate the journey to the present day. Reports from five of the first qualified CSWs who agreed to be interviewed and share their memories and experiences have been included in this book. All those interviewed have continued to work within the areas of sign language and Deafness; four of those interviewed became qualified sign language interpreters and one continued to work as a CSW and as a tutor for Deaf students. Each of the original CSWs interviewed was able to name people who trained as CSWs alongside them and either became sign language interpreters or remained in the field of Deaf education. All those interviewed speak fondly of their training as CSWs and the work they subsequently undertook.

Chris Green, as one of the people who worked to develop the training and role of the CSW, speaks frankly of his experiences of this time. Together with Warren Nickerson, Chris was one of the key people responsible for the evolvement of the CSW. Despite all the criticisms and frustrations involved, Chris remains proud of his involvement and undoubtedly plays a key part in the history of CSWs.

Some of the professionals interviewed were, at times, critical of CSWs and did not agree with the drive for registration. As authors, we were keen to allow contributors to speak freely and express their personal opinions. On more than one occasion we were reminded of the quotation 'I may not approve of what you say, but I will defend to the death your right to say it.' (The origin of this quotation is unclear, but some claim that it was Voltaire). Even though we may not have agreed with some of the sentiments expressed, we were adamant that all contributors should be encouraged to express themselves freely, without fear of contradiction. It was also important to us that we did not make any comment on anyone's contribution. There are always two sides to every story and it is sometimes difficult to appreciate the 'big picture', however by not giving our reactions to reports, we hoped that readers would be able to form their own opinions and perhaps use the reports for debate or further discussion.

We are indebted to all those who contributed to this book and gave their time so freely. It is our belief that this history of CSWs will be more accurate than others due to the fact that it is written by so many people who were 'there' at key stages. All of the contributors play a key part in the history of CSWs and the book would not have been the same without their input

– their stories have helped to make this book unique. Any inaccuracies must be blamed on the passage of time and the effect this has on all of our memories.

The struggle for recognition for CSWs has continued for twenty five years. There is now a nationally recognised level 3 qualification, National Occupational Standards and a firm request for a registration category for CSWs within the National Registers of Communication Professionals with Deaf People. What is needed now is for more people to believe that appropriately trained CSWs are required. We have reached the silver jubilee of the CSW. It is hoped that CSWs will indeed have the recognition they deserve long before the golden jubilee.

The final word must go to Simpson (2007) 'Any system will work if people believe in it. No system will work ...if people don't believe in it.' (Simpson, 2007, p198).

Believe.

Table of Acronymns

ACSW	Association of Communication Support Workers
AGM	Annual General Meeting
ASLI	Association of Sign Language Interpreters
BATOD	British Association of Teachers of the Deaf
BDA	British Deaf Association
BID	Birmingham Institute for the Deaf
BSL	British Sign Language
BTEC	Business and Technicians Education Council
CACDP	Council for the Advancement of Communication with Deaf People

CHESS	Consortium of Higher Education Support Services
CPD	Continuing Professional Development
CSW	Communication Support Worker
DCSF	Department for Children Schools and Families
DESF	Deaf Education Support Forum
DIN	Deaf Interpreters Network
DWEB	Deaf Welfare Examining Board
ECSTRA	Education, Communication, Support, Training, Retraining and Advice for Deaf Adults
ERADE	Exeter Royal Academy for Deaf Education
FE	Further Education
HE	Higher Education
HoSS	Head of Sensory Service
JCQ	Joint Council for Qualifications
LASER	Language of Sign as an Educational Resource
LLUK	Lifelong Learning United Kingdom
LSIS	Learning and Skills Improvement Service
LSP	Learning Support Practitioner
MSC	Manpower Services Commission

NATED	National Association for Tertiary Education for Deaf People
NCSWD	National Council of Social Workers for the Deaf
NOS	National Occupational Standards
NRCPD	National Register of Communication Professionals with Deaf People
OCN	Open College Network
OfQual	Office of Qualifications and Examinations Regulation
RNID	Royal National Institute for the Deaf
SASU	Student Access Support Unit
SSC	Sector Skills Council
ToD	Teacher of the Deaf
TDA	Training and Development Agency for Schools
VLP	Visual Language Professionals
WEEP	Work Experience on Employers Premises
WEP	Work Experience Programme
YOP	Youth Opportunities Programme
YTS	Youth Training Scheme

References

Chapter 1:

British Deaf Association [online] at http://www.bda.org.uk/about-us/bda-history (accessed 2012).

Green, C. and Nickerson, W. (1992) The Rise of the Communicator: A Perspective on Post 16 Education and Training for Deaf People, Moonshine Books, England.

Milan 1880 [online] at www.milan1880.com (accessed 2012).

Signature [online] at http://www.signature.org.uk (accessed 2012).

Simpson, S. (2007) Advance to an Ideal: the fight to raise the standard of communication between Deaf and hearing people, Scottish Workshop Publications, Edinburgh.

Chapter 2:

Derbyshire College of Higher Education (1987) The Working Hands Project Certificate in Deafness Studies: Course Document A Joint European Economic Community/ Derbyshire County Council Initiative.

Derbyshire College of Higher Education (1989) Certificate in Deafness Studies: Course Document A one year full time course, leading to a college certificate in Deafness Studies, for people wishing to work with deaf people in Training, Employment and Post-16 Education, Sponsored by the Employment Department Training Agency.

Chapter 3: No references in document.

Chapter 4:

Ashford, D. E. (1989) Death of a Great Survivor: The Manpower Services Commission in the UK. Governance, Volume 2, Issue 4, pages 365–383, October 1989

Gillard, D. (2011) Education in England: a brief history www.educationengland.org.uk/history (accessed 09.11.2011).

Green, C. and Nickerson, W. (1992) The Rise of the Communicator: A Perspective on Post-16 Education and Training for Deaf People. Moonshine Books.

Scott, D. (1986) The Manpower Services Commission and the Organisation of Non-Statutory Welfare (p81-101)in Brenton, M., editor, The Year Book of Social Policy in Britain 1985-6. Routledge, London.

Simpson, S. (2007) Advance to an Ideal the fight to raise the standard of communication between Deaf and hearing people Scottish Workshop Publications, Edinburgh

Wikipedia. Recession in the United Kingdom http://en.wikipedia.org/wiki/Early_1980s_recession#Recession_in_the_United_Kingdom (accessed 09.11.2011).

Chapter 5: No references in document.

Chapter 6:

Conrad, R. (1979) The Deaf Schoolchild, London: Harper and Row.

Smith, C. (1995) The Return of the Mission? in Deafness Magazine, Issue 1, Volume 11, 1995.

Chapter 7:

ASLI (Association of Sign Language Interpreters) Guidelines for Interpreters Working in Educational Settings [online] at: www.asli.org.uk/asli-s-policies (accessed 2012).

Brien, D., Brown, R and Collins, J. (2002). The Organisation and Provision of British Sign Language/ English Interpreters in England, Scotland and Wales on behalf of the Department of Work and Pensions, HMSO, London.

Brien, D, Brown, R and Collins, J. (2004). Some recommendations regarding the provision and organisation of British Sign Language/ English interpreters in England, Scotland and Wales in Deaf Worlds: International Journal of Deaf studies; Volume 20, issue 1, 2004.

CACDP (2001b). Communication Support Workers: A Code of Professional Practice. CACDP: Durham.

Harrington, F. J. (2001). The Rise, Fall and Re-invention of the Communicator: re-defining roles and responsibilities in educational interpreting in Frank J. Harrington and Graham H. Turner (eds) Interpreting Interpreting: Studies and Reflections on Sign Language Interpreting, Coleford: Douglas McLean, 89-101.

Kernoff, C. (2001). The Reconstruction of the Role of the Communication Support Worker for School Age Children. Unpublished M.A. dissertation: University of Durham.

Chapter 8: No references in document.

Chapter 9: No references in document.

Chapter 10:

Application Guide (2011) Communication Support for D/deaf learners; An Application of the National Occupational Standards for Learning Support Staff who provide Communication Support. (online) at: http://www.signature.org.uk/documents/ Deaf_learners_guide.pdf

Brien, D., Brown, R. and Collins, J. (2002) The Organisation and Provision of British Sign Language/ English Interpreters in England, Scotland and Wales, Department of Work and Pensions, HMSO, London.

Close the Gap (2008) an NDCS campaign, NDCS briefing on educational under achievement by Deaf children in England (online) at: www.publications.parliament.uk/pa/cm2000607/ cmhansard/cm070306/halltext/70306h0011.htm

CRIDE Report 2011 http://www.batod.org.uk/index.php?id=/ publications/survey/CRIDE2011.pdf

Evaluation of the BSL Futures Project, Old Bell 3 for the Welsh Assembly Government (2008) [online] at: www.oldbell3.co.uk

Green, C. (1990) The Communicator, Zeitgeist and Brian, in Deafness Magazine, Issue 1, Volume 6, National Council of Social Workers with Deaf People Magazine.

Green, C. and Nickerson, W. (1992) The Rise of the Communicator: A Perspective on Post 16 Education and Training for Deaf People, Moonshine Books, England.

Harrington, F. J. (2001) The Rise, Fall and Re-invention of the Communicator: re-defining roles and responsibilities in educational interpreting in Frank J. Harrington and Graham H. Turner (eds) Interpreting Interpreting: Studies and Reflections on Sign Language Interpreting, Coleford: Douglas McLean, 89-101.

McLeod, S. A. (2009). Simply Psychology;. Retrieved 2 March 2012, from http://www.simplypsychology.org/piaget.html

Rogers, R. (2000) Communication Support Work Training in the 21st Century (online) at: http://www.online-conference.net/downloads/sdp_free/training_csw_training.pdf

Turner, K. (2006) Communication Support Workers in Publications/BATOD On-line Magazine/Facets of Sign/ Communication Support workers(online) at: http://www.batod. org.uk/index.php?id=/publications/on-linemagazine/sign/csws. htm

Chapter 11: No references in document.

Chapter 12:

Brien, D., Brown, R. and Collins, J. (2002) The Organisation and Provision of British Sign Language/English Interpreters in England, Scotland and Wales A study carried out on behalf of the Department for Work and Pensions By University of Durham. http://statistics.dwp.gov.uk/asd/asd5/IH102.pdf

Calderon, R. (2000). Parental involvement in Deaf children's education programs as a predictor of child's language, early reading, and social-emotional development. Journal of Deaf Studies and Deaf Education, 5:140-155.

Conrad, R. (1979) The Deaf School Child. London: Harper Row.

Blamey, P. J., Sarant, J. Z., Paatsch, L. E., Barry, J. G., Bow, C. P., Wales, R. J., Wright, M., Psarros, C., Rattigan, K and Tooher, R. (2001) Relationships among speech perception, production, language, hearing loss, and age in children with impaired hearing. Journal of Speech, Language, and Hearing Research 44, 264-285.

Fortnum, H. M., Summerfield, A. Q., Marshall, D. H., Davis, A. C. and Bamford, J. M. (2001) Prevalence of permanent childhood hearing impairment in the United Kingdom and implications for universal neonatal hearing screening: questionnaire based ascertainment study. British Medical Journal, 323:536-539. http://www.bmj.com/content/323/7312/536.full

Glasner, Aviva Twersky Western Criminology Review : July 1, (2010).

Gregory, S., Bishop, J., Sheldon, L. (1995) Deaf Young People and their families. Cambridge University Press.

Hindley, P. A., Hill, P. D., McGuigan, S. and Kitson, N. (1994) Psychiatric disorders in Deaf and hard of hearing young people. Journal of Child Psychology and Psychiatry, 34:917-934.
Hindley, P. A. and Kitson, N., eds. 2000. Mental health and Deafness. London: Whurr.

Labour Force Survey, March 2008.

Lamb, B. (2009) Inquiry into Parental Confidence and Special Educational Needs. Department for Education.

Mitchell, R. E., Karchmer, M. A. (2004) Chasing the Mythical Ten Percent: Parental Hearing Status of Deaf and Hard of Hearing Students in the United States. Sign Language Studies. Washington: Winter 2004. Vol. 4, Iss. 2, p.138-163,216-217.

National Occupational Standards Application Guide for CSWs. Signature: http://www.signature.org.uk/documents/Deaf_learners_guide.pdf

Powers, S. (2006) Learning from Success. High achieving Deaf Pupils. RNID and University of Birmingham.

Rall, E. (2007) Psychosocial Development of Children with Hearing Loss. The ASHA Leader. September 25.

Ratna, H. (1996) Counselling Deaf and Hard of Hearing Clients, The BAC Counselling Reader.

Research Findings North West Partnership Bridging the Access Gap Conference 22 November 2008. Learning and Skills Council.

RNID, (2006) Opportunity Blocked, the December 2006 Labour Force Survey.

Support and aspiration: A new approach to special educational needs and disability. Department for Education (2011).

Special Educational Needs 2010: an analysis 19 October 2010 Department for Education.

Wallis, D., Musselman, C. and MacKay, S. (2004) Hearing

mothers and their Deaf children: the relationship between early, on-going mode match and subsequent mental health functioning in adolescents. Journal of Deaf Studies and Deaf Education, 9:2-14.

Woll, B. (2008) Mental Capital and Wellbeing: Making the most of ourselves in the 21st century State-of-Science Review: SR-D5 Deafness and Hearing Impairment.

Chapter 13: No references in document.

Chapter 14:

Brooks, R. (2008). The Mindset of Teachers Capable of Fostering Resilience in Students. Canadian Journal of School Psychology, Vol. 23, No. 1, 114-126.

CILT, the National Centre for Languages, operating as part of the CfBT Education Trust. National Occupational Standards in Interpreting (CILT 2006). http://www.cilt.org.uk/home/standards_and_qualifications/uk_occupational_standards/interpreting.aspx

CRIDE Report 2011 http://www.batod.org.uk/index.php?id=/publications/survey/CRIDE2011.pdf

CSW Code of Practice (2007) http://www.nated.org/DDT_Show_Entry_1F_Documents.asp?GalleryName=NATED_downloads&EntryID=403&ImageSeqNo=1

Harrington, Frank J. (2001) The Rise, Fall and Re-invention of the Communicator: Re-defining Roles and Responsibilities in Educational Interpreting, in Frank J. Harrington and Graham H. Turner (eds) Interpreting Interpreting: Studies and Reflections on Sign Language Interpreting, Coleford: Douglas McLean, 89-101.

Joint Council for Qualifications. Access Arrangements, Reasonable Adjustments and Special Considerations. With effect from 1st September 2011 to 31st August 2012. http://www.jcq.org.uk

National Occupation Standards for Learning Support Practitioners CSWs (2009) http://www.excellencegateway.org.uk/node/17223

National Occupation Standards: An Application of the National Occupational Standards for Learning Support Staff who provide Communication Support (2010) [online] at: http://www.signature.org.uk/documents/deaf_learners_guide.pdf

Segal, J. (1988) Teachers Have Enormous Power in Affecting a Child's Self-Esteem. The Brown University Child Behavior [sic] and Development Newsletter, 4, 1-3.

Signature (2009) Report prepared by Signature on behalf of the LSC in the North West and the North West Partnership. Research Findings from the 'Bridging the Access Gap Conference', 22 November 2008. http://www.signature.org.uk/news.php?news_id=37 Downloaded 22nd June 2009.

Chapter 15: No references in document.

Chapter 16:

Disability Discrimination Act (1995) [online] http://www.legislation.gov.uk/ukpga/1995/50/contents (accessed 29/03/2012).

Green, C. and Nickerson, W. (1992) The Rise of the Communicator: A Perspective on Post-16 Education and Training for Deaf People, Moonshine Books, England.

Simpson, S. (2007) Advance to an Ideal: the fight to raise the standard of communication between Deaf and hearing people. Edinburgh, Scottish Workshop Publications.

The Year 1987 from the People History [online] http://www.thepeoplehistory.com/1987.html (accessed 28/03/2012).